Mother-Talk
Conversations with Mothers
of Lesbian Daughters
and FTM Transgender Children

Sarah F. Pearlman

T0158574

Mother-Talk
Conversations with Mothers
of Lesbian Daughters
and FTM Transgender Children

Sarah F. Pearlman

DEMETER

DEMETER PRESS

Published by:
Demeter Press
c/o Motherhood Initiative for Research and
 Community Involvement (MIRCI)
140 Holland St. West, P.O. 13022
Bradford, ON, L3Z 2Y5
Telephone: 905.775.9089
Email: info@demeterpress.org
Website: www.demeterpress.org

Demeter Press logo based on Skulptur "Demeter" by Maria-Luise Bodirsky
<www.keramik-atelier.bodirsky.edu>

Cover Artwork: Mary Lou Nye
Cover/Interior Design: Luciana Ricciutelli

Printed and Bound in Canada

Library and Archives Canada Cataloguing in Publication

Pearlman, Sarah F.
        Mother-talk : conversations with mothers of lesbian daughters and FTM transgender children / Sarah F. Pearlman.

Includes bibliographical references.
ISBN 978-1-927335-05-5

        1. Mothers—United States—Interviews. 2. Parents of gays—United States—Interviews. 3. Parents of transsexuals—United States—Interviews. 4. Mothers and daughters—United States. 5. Lesbians—Family relationships—United States. 6. Transsexuals—Family relationships—United States. 7. Transgender people—Family relationships—United States. I. Title.

HQ759.9145.P42 2012   306.874'30973   C2012-901694-2

To those I love

My Children:
my son, Richard Epstein and my daughter, Barbara Pearlman

My grandchildren:
Kelsey Pearlman-Marriott, Jenna Mollie Pearlman-Marriott,
Ariel Epstein, Rogers Epstein, and Owen Theodore Smith

My family:
Janice Epstein, Noah Smith, Lois Winnick, Ian Winnick,
Susan Tarren Pearlman, Mitchell Pearlman, and Shane Marriott

To Gloria Charles who helped make it possible.

To the memory of my long-time friend, Carol Capizzi.

And, especially, to my mother, Mollie Bromberg Pearlman
… who made this book happen.

And of course,
to all the mothers of lesbian daughters and
FTM transgender children that
I met and interviewed—who are the book.

What can I say, but that it's not easy?
I cannot lift the stones out of your way,
And I can't cry your bitter tears for you.
I would if I could, what can I say?

But we're not one, we're worlds apart.
You and I,
Child of my body, bone of my bone,
Apple of my eye.

And like a young tree, I see you sway and bend,
And I'm so afraid, afraid you might break,
Tossed by the wind, the storms that come your way,
And careless strangers, seeing fruit, who reach out to
     take …

But we're not one, we're worlds apart.

—Rosalie Sorrels, excerpt from lyrics to "Apple of my Eye."

Table of Contents

Preface   xi

Acknowledgements   xiii

Introduction   1

DEVASTATION

1. Hannah: That Child Always Gave Me Trouble   19
2. Edie: I Hate Myself for How I Behaved   23
3. Sara: She Wasn't Going To Be The Nice Little Lesbian
   I Hoped She Would Be   29
4. Karen: Gay Was A Piece of Cake   36
5. Anna: Why Would You Want To Be a White Male?   45

LOSS

6. Elise: She's a Guy Now   57
7. Mariam: All Those Weddings, All Those Showers   66
8. Jenny: He's Gonna Lose Everything Except His Parents   70
9. Lisa: I Miss The Person He Was When He Was a She   77

ADOLESCENCE

10. Debra: I Felt Helpless As A Mother   91

11. Rina: Mom, That's Me, I Am a Boy, Inside I Am a Boy 100
12. Beth: I Just Don't Like Labels 111

NOT THE ONLY ISSUE

13. Lila: I Regret the Kind of Mother I Was 119
14. Fran: She Took Me on a Ride I Wasn't Prepared For 125
15. Naomi: Parents Do Leave Kids on Hillsides 131
16. Cheryl: Her Lesbianism Is Third in Line 140

CONNECTION

17. Shirley: God, Watch Over Her For Me, Everyday 149
18. Lois: Whatever Kind of Relationship He Wants To
      Have, We Will Have 159
19. Eleanor: If You Can't Be Supportive, Don't
      Be Around 168
20. Annemarie: You Can't Hide a Baby 174
21. Lillian: My Child Is Not an Abomination 179

ACTIVISM

22. Marie: She Made Me More of a Person 185
23. Judith: I Have a Much Happier Son Than I Ever
      Did a Daughter 193
24. Martha: Just Expect To See Somebody That Looks
      Like Your Former Daughter's Twin Brother 201

Appendices 210

Preface

I told my mother that I was a lesbian a year before she died. Unprepared for her reaction, I never anticipated how furious she would be, or that she would barely speak to me during the months that followed. I had no idea if she told anyone and aside from one futile attempt to talk, I conformed to her wish for silence. It was clear that I had upset her enough. My mother gradually became less distant and there were occasional moments of warmth and affection as if telling her had never happened. But our relationship was never quite the same. I never knew what she thought or what the twists and turns of her feelings were—or if she had somehow come to terms with having a lesbian daughter. I did not think that she might have been frightened for me and there were many times that I would have gladly taken back the words I spoke. Her death, following a brief illness, ensured that I could speculate but never really know. It was hearing other mothers that helped me understand my own mother's experience of grief and disconnection, and her predictable struggle and inability to make the journey towards acceptance.

Acknowledgements

My heart-felt appreciation to Daphna Amit, RoseAnne Bilodeau, Gloria Charles, Shani Dowd, Donna Fleischer, Roberta Issler, Chloe Karl, Mara Keller, Loraine Obler, George Thomson, Jane Tuohy, and Loretta Wrobel. Some of you for reading early drafts, all for tolerating my various laments and believing that I could write this book—and all for our great conversations on mothers, daughters, gender, transgender—and just about everything else. I love you all.

And especially Kathy McCloskey and Alice Fisher who did all of the above and more. I love you both.

Thanks to my marketing friend, Sue Reamer, to Rowena Winik, Maxine Schuster, and Jan Taylor for last minute editing, and to Toni Amato, my writing coach and consultant. Without him, *Mother-Talk* would have been a different book.

Thanks to Esther Rothblum for her many, many years of help, support and belief in me, to David Singer who opened so many doors to my professional life, and to Adele Hurowitz for looking over an early draft. It was Adele's suggestions that turned *Mother-Talk* into the book it is.

Much appreciation and thanks to Byran Hoffman for technological comfort, computer brilliance, and emergency help, and Mary Lou Nye for her great artwork.

And to all the wonderful people connected to Demeter Press for their help, support, and patience: Randy Chase, Luciana Ricciutelli, Renée Knapp, Angie Deveau, and Tracey Carlyle.

And especially to Andrea O'Reilly for her pioneering role and leadership in establishing motherhood studies and mothering as a discipline and subject to be researched and respected—and her enthusiasm and dedication in bringing *Mother-Talk* to print.

Introduction

Quando si ha un figlio, non sai che ti invitano en casa.
—Sicilian folk saying*

It was in 1990, four years after my mother's death, when I began to interview mothers of lesbians. Most of these women had learned of their daughters' sexual orientation in the mid-1980s, a time when concealment of sexual orientation, exaggerated stereotypes, and beliefs that lesbianism was abnormal or deviant prevailed. There were few parent support groups—mostly in large cities—no gay-straight alliances for lesbian and gay youth, no civil unions, and no positive gay characters in any television series or movies. No wonder that most of the women I interviewed in 1990, like my own mother, finding out a daughter was a lesbian was a devastating crisis.

Ten years later, I began to think about additional interviews. I was curious if parents were reacting differently when lesbians and gay men were more visible, when lesbians were having babies, and when there was greater acceptance of gay relationships and civil rights. As I began to seek out mothers to interview, I came in contact with a new group altogether. These were mothers who had learned that their children identified as transgender and had, or were transitioning to male. Although these mothers' experiences were similar in many ways to mothers of gay children, there were many differences. Both parents of gay and transgender children have numerous fears and concerns, most often focused on the potential for violence and threat to physical safety. However, while

1

mothers of lesbian daughters may struggle with changed expectations, they still have a daughter. Mothers of female-to-male (FTM) transgender children have a more life-altering experience—and a more complex and difficult course of adjustment compounded by greater shame—as well as the actual loss of a daughter. As one mother of an FTM child, once identified as a lesbian, said, "A lesbian is nothing. My daughter's gone. She's just not there anymore."

I was struck by the enormity of what these women were asked to accept. Many were overwhelmed by confusion and grief as they watched daughters transition and become increasingly masculine. Yet some seemed to fully accept their transgender child and had become activists on behalf of other parents as well as engaging in the fight for transgender civil rights. Still others recognized cross-gender identity in their young children, helping them to express themselves as the gender they felt they were. When one mother suggested that I interview her, the idea of an additional study took shape, one on mothers of children that had, or were changing sex to male.

The Interviews/The Stories

The twelve mothers of lesbians I interviewed in 1990 lived in New York, Connecticut, Massachusetts, and New Hampshire. All were Caucasian and heterosexual, and most had heard of my study through local chapters of Parents and Friends of Lesbians and Gays (PFLAG). All interviews were conducted in person and most took place in the mothers' homes. However, in 2000-2001, my search for mothers had a "snowball" effect of the Internet and I received numerous e-mail inquiries from mothers around the United States, as well as from Canada, England, and Australia, who had learned of my study through PFLAG and various trans families and LGBT web sites and list serves. Although I had planned to interview each woman in person, it was difficult to find a sufficient number of mothers of FTM transgender children who lived nearby on the East Coast and I decided to mail instructions and questions to several mothers who lived at a distance, have them tape their responses, and return the tapes to me.[1]

The mothers in 2000-2001 included women from Connecticut, Massachusetts, New York, New Jersey, Virginia, Illinois, Ohio, Texas, Washington State, Alaska, Canada, and Australia. All identified as heterosexual, one woman was partnered with an FTM trans man, and all, except for one African-Caribbean woman, were Caucasian since I was unable to find other ethnic-racial minority women interested in being interviewed. Most interviews took place in the mothers' homes; others in offices, hotel rooms, or restaurants. Once transcribed, I re-wrote the transcripts as stories—omitting repetition and digressions, and re-organizing so that the mothers' narratives would be more readable—but always in the words of the mothers. Although some of the activist mothers may be recognizable, all names as well as other possible identifying information were changed in order to protect the identity of the mothers and their children since several mothers, especially those of transgender children, expressed concern that if their identity was not disguised, their children might be outed.

Mother-Talk is an anthology of stories of twenty-four mothers[2,3]—twelve whose daughters were lesbians and twelve whose children had, or were intending to transition. Of those twelve, eight were mothers of children who first came out as lesbians. There is a strong dividing—and frequently divisive—line between lesbians who experience themselves as women, and those who called themselves lesbians before transition, but who identified as male. For those individuals who transitioned, but were lesbians for a time, it was because of same-sex attraction since lesbianism was the one identity and category available to them, and lesbian communities the one welcoming place and only home. That is, until hormonal treatments and surgical technologies emerged that made FTM sex reassignment possible along with an increase of information (e.g., media and Internet) and individuals supporting transition.

It was not my intention that *Mother-Talk* be a scholarly book, but rather a collection of stories of mothers who were willing to share highly personal information about themselves and their children. Through interview questions (see Appendices: The Interviews), these women were asked to think back and construct a narrative or story about a time that—for most—changed their lives. It was the mothers, their words, and their descriptions of their experiences that provided an in-depth and insightful understanding of the complexity of learning and adapting to a daughter who was a lesbian, or a child who had, or was planning to change sex—providing a much fuller picture than more traditional research methods.

Divided into sections entitled, *Devastation, Loss, Not the Only Issue, Adolescence, Keeping the Connection,* and *Activism* that capture the major themes, the book begins with the story of a mother still unable to come to terms with her daughter's lesbianism. In a later story, an African-Caribbean woman—determined to be part of her child's world—attends a PFLAG meeting five days after learning her daughter is gay while another mother sets aside her own feelings of distress and helps her adolescent daughter find her way into the world of gay youth. A Lebanese-American woman mourns a two-fold loss: the first an anticipated relationship with her daughter, now a lesbian, who had chosen a different life path; the second, the likely estrangement of her family and community should they discover her daughter's sexual orientation. Yet, another woman relates that when substance abuse, self-cutting, and depression are present, the sexual orientation of a daughter may no longer be the primary issue. One mother, a nationally-known trans activist, calls transition a "blessing" that transformed their once difficult and unlikable FTM son into a likable and caring person while another, also a well-known trans activist, wishes she still had a daughter. Still another woman recalled that her child played more like a boy than a girl, but questions why he wanted to be a male when, as a lesbian, he had been so critical of men. Finally, many stories recounted the mothers' journeys from initial devastation to political activism—first on behalf of other parents and then the civil rights of all LGBT people—enriching their lives and changing their view of the world.

Mothers of Lesbian Daughters

Most of the mothers I interviewed in 1990—and those I interviewed in 2000-2001 who learned a daughter was a lesbian before 1990—grew up in conventional environments. The majority learned of their children's sexual orientation when they were adults, were unaware of any gay relatives, and if they had any exposure to gay people, it was mostly gay men. Almost all believed the prevalent stereotypes that lesbians had short-lived and unhappy relationships, led tragic and lonely lives, and that they were women who simultaneously hated but wanted to be men. No wonder that most of these mothers experienced disclosure as a crisis, describing feelings of shock and devastation that affected them for a long period of time. As one mother told me, "I cried all day. I cried for weeks." Another said, "I couldn't feel worse if she died." While these mothers did express fears as to their daughters' safety, most related that their own feelings, at least initially, took precedence. What were central were feelings of sorrow, loss, and shame as what others, if they knew, would think of them as parents. Many grieved the bridal showers and wedding celebrations that would not happen and—unless they anticipated grandchildren from other children—mourned that they would not be grandmothers. Disclosure of sexual orientation also brought about disturbing sexual imagery and some mothers said that, for a time, they lost all interest in sex. As one mother related, "I don't want to sleep with my husband anymore. I mean have sex with him ... when he tries, I think of my daughter. I think of women having sex together. I can't help it."

Nearly all of the women interviewed said that their daughter's lesbianism was a total surprise. Yet, many recalled that they had noticed signs, but it was only after disclosure that they connected daughters' behaviors to sexual orientation. Several stated that daughters had been tomboys during childhood and adolescence (confusing lesbianism with masculinity). Others related that daughters were engaging in feminist activities, making anti-male statements, were disinterested in dating men, living in households with lesbians, or becoming more masculine in appearance. Most hoped that it was a stage, thinking they hadn't met the right man and that they would eventually return to heterosexuality. One mother said the following: "Maybe there just weren't enough available men that she could meet. So I actually called up a dating service. I paid one hundred dollars for the dating service...." Hoping that a daughter's lesbianism was temporary helped many of these women to cope as they struggled to adjust.

Almost all mothers attempted to identify causes or explanations for their daughter's lesbianism. Most questioned their own mothering, concerned that they had done something wrong and not been good mothers—echoing psychological theories that family relationships, especially mothers, caused homosexuality. As example, one mother thought perhaps her daughter needed "love from a woman that she hadn't gotten from me." Others wondered if dominating fathers had turned daughters against men, or that something bad had happened to them such as sexual assault. Some had a more self-involved view, thinking that daughters might have become lesbians to rebel, be different from them, or to hurt them. Said one mother, "I kept asking myself why did she want to hurt me? She could have kept it to herself." Yet although distressed, most mothers sought information; many joined PFLAG within a year and a half of disclosure, and several became involved in outreach to other parents of lesbians and gay men.

By 1990, lesbians and gay men had become much more visible. Civil unions were taking place and there was increasing acceptance of gay relationships. Homosexuality had become much more a part of public consciousness as a result of the increase in available information (e.g., media and Internet), out media celebrities, and television portrayals of lesbians and gay men's lives—a phenomena referred to as the "visibility revolution" (Savin-Williams vii). Also, more individuals were recognizing sexual orientation at younger ages and more gay adolescents were self-identifying and disclosing to parents, and were less troubled about their sexual orientation depending on where they lived, the schools they attended, religious values, and expectation of parental acceptance.

As compared to the mothers in 1990, most of the mothers interviewed in 2000-2001 learned of their daughters' lesbianism during adolescence, were aware of gay relatives, were acquainted with many more gay people, had close friends who were lesbians, knew that lesbians were having babies (two mothers had grandchildren by lesbian daughters), and disclosed to friends and family members more quickly. Reactions to disclosure of sexual orientation also varied. Many said that although they experienced initial feelings of shock and grief, these reactions were more short-lived with concerns mostly focused on the safety and well-being of their daughters. Other mothers described a concerned but less troubled reaction, quickly understanding that this was who their daughter truly was. These mothers, especially, ascribed to child-rearing values that encouraged individuality and the right to individual identity and self-expression. They wanted to be involved in their child's lives and tended to offer immediate help and support, especially if daughters were adolescents and living at home—suppressing their own feelings and behaving in ways they thought were in the best interest of their child. If they did join PFLAG, it was not so much for themselves, but rather for information and assistance in order to be helpful to their daughters.

Like those interviewed in 1990, all of the mothers in 2000-2001 expressed multiple concerns about the costs of breaking social norms, but safety was the primary issue. Citing gay bashing and threats against gay people, many feared the possibility of physical attack and some brought up Matthew Shepard who had become a symbol of danger to a gay child. Still, several mothers expressed admiration of their daughters as well as admiration and respect for the closeness and affection they had observed in lesbian couples, and a few said that their lives were greatly enriched as a result of having a lesbian daughter.

Mothers of FTM Transgender Children

Although reactions varied in intensity, the majority of mothers of FTM transgender children described that learning about their child's intended transition caused a profound crisis characterized by shock, disorientation, and grief. Several had observed that their daughter's appearance was becoming increasingly masculine, but because they had initially identified as lesbians, mothers thought that changes in appearance were due to a butch lesbian identity, or as experimentation with self-expression. Consequently, nearly all were taken completely by surprise and most had never heard of FTM transgenderism. As one mother told me, "I didn't have a clue. I never heard of it. You're what! You're not really a she. You're a he. How could that happen? I was in horror." Another who guessed said, "At age fifteen, she told me she wanted to be a boy and have a sex change. I was so angry. I said well, yeah, well, you do that, but right now you're a girl so get over it."

Almost all of the mothers described a prolonged period of devastation and shame as well as confusion on how to comprehend or tell others about a daughter's transition. Most concealed it, some for a long time, with major concerns as to how others might react. Many doubted the authenticity of a daughter's male identity—openly challenging their daughter's decision to change sex. Nearly all hoped that it was just a phase and that transition would "go away," and one woman said that she pretended her daughter's transition was a sex role change rather than an actual physical body change. Similar to the mothers of lesbian daughters, denial of the permanence of transition helped these women to cope as they struggled to understand and come to terms with sex reassignment. Yet most sought information and support, and one woman told how she located an online group that changed her life as she found other mothers of FTMs, saying "I felt so connected to other people who were undergoing the same experience and all of them seemed to be as shocked and stunned that this was happening to them as I was." However, another mother, an Australian woman, immediately became her young trans son's advocate, saying, "My job was to minimize the trauma, the hassles, and smooth the way, make his life as easy as I could. It's a mother's job."

All of these mothers had to tolerate secrecy and concealment, at least for a time, and all had numerous fears and concerns such as discrimination or psychological damage resulting from insults, harassment, or exclusion; worries that included the long-term consequences of testosterone and the danger of surgery—and if their child would ever be acceptable as romantic and sexual partners. But hate crimes and physical violence were clearly the most prevalent fears. Similar to Matthew Shepard, many mothers spoke of the movie, *Boys Don't Cry* and Brandon Teena as a frightening symbol representing what could happen to a transgender child—well aware that gender-variant people were the most vulnerable and most frequently targeted group for persecution and violence. Safety, especially in public bathrooms, was a major issue, and mothers, once reconciled to transition, experienced great relief when they saw their child could successfully pass as male. Those whose children identified as gay males expressed the most intense fears, specifically about the threat of physical violence and contracting AIDS.

Nearly all mothers recalled cross-gender behaviors as far back as early childhood, describing that daughters preferred boys' activities and hated to be dressed in girls' clothing. Some had told them that they wanted to be boys; others believed they were boys, and a few had chosen boys' names. One woman said, "She wouldn't play with dolls. She wanted to urinate standing up." Other mothers expressed that there was something about their daughters' personalities that were more stereotypically male: more independent with less need for closeness—or that they played like boys and had more interest in activities and ideas than feelings or emotions. Many had viewed their daughters as feminists or tomboys and several had thought that masculine-like behaviors might be an early sign of lesbianism.

Recollections of childhood and adolescence gave credibility to transition, helping mothers to make sense of sex reassignment and paving the way for eventual acceptance. A number said that they eventually realized that problems experienced during childhood and adolescence were due to gender concerns. Others expressed regrets that they had pushed their daughters to become more feminine, and did not understand, or were unaware of their daughter's male identity. As one mother related, "I understand now why she was so unhappy and had so many problems." Said another, "It all felt so bogus. It felt like it was all a lie. Like I was duped. I didn't really know my own child.... What kind of mother was I?"

Once disclosed, the majority of trans sons continued to maintain contact with their mothers, usually through e-mail or by telephone and most were empathic and responsive to their mother's confusion and concerns. However, a few mothers did report that contact was infrequent for a time. One speculated that, "When [he] started to transition, he kind of pulled away.... He needed his space to get comfortable and I was probably asking more questions than he wanted to deal with." A second said her child was "...furious with us. I've seen it in other transgender individuals too. Some of it's adolescent separation. But the other is just this rage that nobody really understood [him]."

Because most transgender sons lived a distance away from

their families, changes in appearance, especially once hormonal treatment had begun, was a shock to many mothers. One told me, "I had left really a girl, a gay girl, and now have somebody with some facial hair and a big neck. But after a while, it's still your child." But it was surgery, primarily breast reconstruction that was the turning point—convincing mothers of their child's resolve and reconciling them to the permanence of transition. As physical changes took place, mothers' perception of their child's gender started to change and nearly all began to view and experience their daughter as male. One said, "She looked like a man, her voice, the muscles. I began to see her as a man." A second woman stated that her child "walked down the stairs one summer and he had the hairiest legs I'd ever seen and threw me into shock. He had man's legs. That was the moment that propelled me forward." However, most mothers remained troubled for a long time, but concealed their distress in order to minimize tension and maintain a relationship with their child.

Prior to transition, two transgender sons who had been married and identified as heterosexual remained attracted to men; a third was in a relationship with another FTM individual and all three identified as gay men. Some who had identified as lesbians continued to be involved with women and were perceived as straight. Thus, transition changed perception of sexual orientation, not sexual orientation. However, two who had previously identified as lesbians were in relationships with other trans men and others began to refer to themselves as bisexual. These changes were highly disturbing and disorienting—at least initially—to most mothers. As one woman commented, "I guess any stereotypes left in my brain have all been completely dismantled because I no longer predict anything at all about gender and sexual orientation when it comes to [my child]."

As mothers struggled to describe the experience of transition, several used the metaphor of death. However, it was the specific loss of a daughter and the special importance of the mother-daughter relationship that was the most painful aspect of transition—depriving them of companionship, closeness, and activities they had once shared. One mother told me the following: "We were in the bedroom talking and I started getting undressed. He said,

'Mom, I'm not the same daughter you used to have. You probably shouldn't undress in front of me.' I said, well, you're still my kid. Don't look if you don't want to see." Feelings connected to the loss of a daughter persisted even among those who were most active in the transgender civil rights movement. As one remarked, "We lost a beautiful daughter. We have a great new son, but we really did lose a daughter. We're out there rah-rahing our new sons, organizing on our soapboxes, but we miss our daughters." For many of the women interviewed, the dream of having a daughter and a deeply entwined relationship that would provide ongoing intimacy, mutual nurturance, and a shared life slowly faded.

While mothers of lesbians tended to focus on family relationships as the cause of same-sex attraction, most mothers of FTMs came to believe that genetics, specifically the amount of androgen secreted during early pregnancy—commonly referred to as the "androgen wash"—affected brain development and explained transgenderism. Several spoke of their child as being born in the wrong body. Others, however, began to believe that gender identity, rather than dichotomous, occurred on a continuum from female to male and was a form of normal variability. As one mother described, "It's a sliding scale from being born male, being born female, being born male moving to female." Another very simply said she believed that "God wanted him to be the way he is and that he is being true to himself."

All of the mothers had initial difficulty and most had ongoing problems with male pronouns. Some explained it as a matter of habit while others said that the change in pronouns confirmed the permanence of transition. All referred to their children as transgender, an all encompassing or umbrella term that refers to all gender-variant people. However, some used the term trans-sexual, once sex reassignment surgery had taken place. But their language was varied and inconsistent. Most alternated between saying daughter or son and she or he—referring to their child as a daughter prior to transition—and sometimes as son following sex reassignment. However, almost all expressed that they had difficulty thinking of their child as a son.

For most of the mothers, acceptance—more often resignation—of transition was a slow, uneven, and ambivalent journey—one that took resolve and hard effort accompanied by the reemergence of anger and grief. Yet nearly all ultimately began to view their trans sons—once transitioned—as happier and better adjusted. A number remarked on the respect and admiration that they had for transsexuals; others expressed that their beliefs and values had undergone transformations and that their lives were enriched as a result of having a transgender son. Mothers involved with transgender people and/or the transgender movement, in particular, became parental role models and surrogate parent figures for other trans individuals. As one woman said, "Everyone wants me to be their mother."

Mother-Talk

The thread linking all of the stories was motherhood and the complex relationship between mothers and daughters as these women related the special meaning of having a daughter, how they had wanted to mother, and their experience of being mothered by their own mothers. Almost all expressed regrets over how they had mothered when their children were young and several spoke of their relationships with their own mothers and its influence on their parenting. Some described an emotionally close relationship that they wanted to repeat with their own daughter while others sought to mother in ways that they had wished they been parented by their mothers—at times deliberately different when it was their own turn to mother. For mothers of transgender children, especially, losing a daughter deprived them of continuing to re-experience their relationship with their own mother, or the opportunity to re-do how they had been mothered.

Nearly all of the mothers wanted a close relationship, intent on remaining connected to their children. Many times their children's feelings took precedence over their own experience of struggle and readiness to accept. For several, there seemed no limits on unconditional love, or limits on children's choices as to how to lead their lives—or limitations on children's expectations of acceptance, no matter what their life decisions. Some accepted whatever relationship was possible; a connection that often depended upon their child's preferences and terms. Said one mother, "Whatever relationship I can have, that's what I will have. Even if it could only be in postcards or only on the phone...."

The women who I interviewed—both in 1990 and 2000-2001—shared many characteristics. The majority was educated beyond the high school level, most had completed college and several had attained advanced degrees. Many had been involved in progressive or social justice causes—causes that included the environment, anti-war, anti-nuclear, and civil rights. Several were affiliated with religious groups that valued diversity and human rights. Those who were members of more conservative churches or congregations (Catholic, fundamentalist Protestant) challenged religious teachings on homosexuality and formulated their own spiritual convictions. Most identified as feminists, or said that they were concerned with women's issues, most specifically the right to abortion and equality of opportunity for women. Nearly all were members of PFLAG and other parents' groups, several in leadership roles in outreach to other parents as well as LGBT civil rights.

Many mothers, however, are unable to oppose or break-away from conventional or religious beliefs on gender and sexuality. Some dependent upon children to reflect them positively to the world remain embarrassed and ashamed, focused on how they might be regarded as parents. Other mothers may be less invested in relationships with children and seem able to reject or disown a gay or trans child. These mothers were not likely to want to be interviewed or be part of a network that would hear of my study and so their voices remain unheard. Although many mothers will find themselves in *Mother-Talk*, the themes and concerns described cannot be applicable to a wider population of mothers of lesbian daughters or FTM transgender children.

Although the interviews took place in 1990 and 2000-2001, the mothers' stories continue to have meaning and relevance to the mothers of today. While many parents can now accept a gay child more easily, others still have difficulty coming to terms with a daughter's lesbianism—and most certainly a child's plan to transition (Kreiger). Parents too are finding that children are expressing and experimenting with more recent identities such as queer,[4] genderqueer,[5] and polyamorous[6]—testing both willingness and capacity for understanding and acceptance. Consequently, there will be new questions for future researchers to ask as mothers continue to be challenged by children exploring new sexual and gender identities. There are also other voices that have not yet been represented—especially those of racial-ethnic minority mothers whose experience and specific concerns need to be heard—and stories yet to be told.

My hope is that *Mother-Talk* will bring about a deeper appreciation of the challenge to comprehend and accept a child who will live a life outside of social norms—and the complexity of coming to terms with the loss of a daughter who has changed sex, or the loss of an anticipated relationship with a daughter, now a lesbian, who has different interests and will lead a different life. I hope too that this book will make a significant contribution to the fields of lesbian, gay, transgender, motherhood, family, and gender studies—informing clinical practice and helping other mothers as well as lesbian daughters and FTM trans children to understand their own mothers, their changed lives, and their determination to remain connected.

The mothers who volunteered to be interviewed were an extraordinary group of women. Most had struggled to remain supportive, and although grieving the loss of a heterosexual daughter, or a child transitioning to male, set aside their own feelings to try to make a better world, not only for their own child, but for all LGBT people—transforming themselves in the process. Nearly all of the stories I listened to touched upon my own experience—as a lesbian, a daughter, and a mother—and many of the interviews quickly turned into mother-to-mother conversations as we talked about our children and reflected upon our own experience of mothering. To this day, I remain amazed by the mothers I met and the stories I heard—the overriding concern for a child's safety and happiness, the unwavering drive to nurture and protect, that tenacious maternal persistence to remain connected to a child—and the determination not to live worlds apart.

*When you have a child, you don't know who you invite into the house.

[1]The mothers interviewed in both 1990 and 2000-2001 were selected in the order in which they contacted me and met the criteria of being a mother of a lesbian daughter or an FTM transgender child.
[2]The interviews and mothers referred to below were those included in *Mother-Talk*.
[3]Choosing those I found to be the most insightful, forthcoming, and interesting stories and that represented the most diversity, I selected three of twelve mothers interviewed in 1990, nine of the sixteen mothers of lesbian daughters, and twelve of the eighteen mothers of FTM transgender children interviewed in 2000-2001 to be included in the book.
[4]One definition of queer refers to those people who do not identify exclusively as heterosexual; another to those who refuse to be categorized as lesbian, gay, bisexual or transgender, who insist on the freedom to define themselves and emphasize their difference from sexual and gender norms—choosing sexual partners as they wish and expressing gender identity (female, male, or both) they feel they are at different times.
[5]Genderqueer refers to those individuals who question gender as a defining category, refuse to be labeled as female or male, and blend and/or change gender identities they feel they are at different times.
[6]One definition of polyamorous refers to those individuals who engage in or commit to two or more sexual/romantic relationships at the same time.

Works Cited

Boenke, Mary, ed. *Trans forming Families: Real Stories about Transgendered Loved Ones*. Hardy, VA: Oak Knoll Press, 1999.

Borhek, Mary. *Coming Out to Parents*. New York: Pilgrim Press, 1983.

Brown, Mildred, and Chloe Rounsley. *True Selves: Understanding Transsexualism*. San Francisco, CA: Jossey-Bass, 1996.

Cromwell, Jason. *Transmen and FTMs: Identities, Bodies, Genders & Sexualities*. Urbana: University of Illinois Press, 1999.

Devor, Holly. *FTM: Female-to-Male Transsexuals in Society*. Bloomington: University of Indiana Press, 1997.

Fairchild, Betty and Nancy Hayward. *Now That You Know: What Every Parent Should Know about Homosexuality*. Now York: Harcourt Brace Javanovich, 1979.

Kreiger, Irwin. *Helping Your Transgender Teen: A Parents Guide*. New Haven, CT: Genderwise Press, 2011.

Muller, Ann. *Parents Matter: Parents' Relationship with Lesbian Daughters and Gay Sons*. Tallahassee, FL: The Naiad Press, Inc., 1987.

Rafkin, Louise. *Different Daughters: A Book by Mothers of Lesbians*. San Francisco. CA: Cleis Press, 1987.

Savin-Williams, Ritch. *Mom, Dad, I'm Gay: How Families Negotiate Coming Out*. Washington, DC: American Psychological Association, 2001.

Sorrels, Rosalie, ed. "Apple of My Eye." *Women, and Who, Myself, I Am; An Anthology of Songs and Poetry of Women's Experience*. Sonoma, CA: Wooden Shoe, 1974.

DEVASTATION

1

Hannah

THAT CHILD ALWAYS GAVE ME TROUBLE

YOU WANT TO KNOW WHAT I FELT. It was one of the worst things that ever happened to me. It was one of the worst days of my life. I was just devastated. I was shocked, but strangely enough, I wasn't surprised. It had crossed my mind. I saw the signs. Sharon never talked about boyfriends. When I went to her house, there were always women around. Boyish women. I said to myself, "It's not possible." She had been married. She always had boyfriends growing up. When she came over, I knew right away that she had something to tell me. The way she was acting. She doesn't just drop in. My first thought was that she was going to tell me that she was living with a man. I even said that to her. I wanted her to know that I wasn't as old-fashioned as I used to be. That it was okay with me. I thought maybe she was settling down. Maybe now she'd want children. Some joke. She probably thought I was a fool.

So she told me. She said, "Mom, I'm a lesbian." Everything after that was a blur. I saw her crying, but I didn't say anything. I wasn't going to comfort her. I didn't need to know this. She didn't have to tell me. That child always gave me trouble. Always into something. Marching here. Marching there. A feminist. Whatever that is! Dressing like she was a teenager. Out of all my children, she was the one I always worried about. And now this. I asked her why she told me and she said something about wanting an honest relationship. Now I remember what I said. I said, "Good. Now we have an honest relationship." I just wanted her to leave. She left.

I cried all day. I cried for weeks. She kept calling me. Maybe twice a week. But there was nothing to say. Nothing I wanted to say to her. Maybe I wanted to get back at her. I was so angry. I kept asking myself, "Why did she want to hurt me?" She could have kept it to herself. I kept thinking about how could I tell anyone? What would they think? I didn't understand the whole thing. It wasn't normal. I thought it was the most terrible thing in the world. I didn't think anything worse could happen to me. In my day, no one talked about it. I knew nothing. Nothing. I thought maybe other people had influenced her. Maybe it was her father. He wasn't an easy man. Now they call it abuse, but he never hit me or anything. I thought maybe she was mixed up in some way. That something bad had happened to her. That something made her against men. I thought maybe it would pass.

My other children knew something was wrong, but I just couldn't talk about it. I did say something to my oldest daughter. But it didn't help. She was pretty upset too. After that I never told anyone. I never told my family. I never told my friends. That is until this one friend, my closest, saw how upset I was and asked me what was wrong. She was the one that found out about PFLAG. She said it might help me to meet other parents. I'm not the type that goes to groups. But I went. That's where I heard about your interviews. I didn't stay long. I just couldn't. I never even introduced myself. When they stopped for coffee, I left. I went home. They were nice people, but I didn't want to hear what they were saying. My lesbian daughter this. My lesbian daughter that. I didn't much like that it was in a church either. Even if it was the basement. Maybe you can help me understand.

My children were my life. Maybe that's what you do when you don't have such a good husband. Have a bad marriage. Maybe that was a mistake. I never understood this daughter. My other children were like me. Like our family. She was different. I couldn't understand why she was so different. After all, I raised her the same as the others. Her divorce was bad enough. That she didn't seem to want children. The older she got, the more selfish she got. Always doing just what she wanted, when she wanted. Where I come from, children are supposed to make you proud. Bring you joy. Not bring you shame. I don't know anything about her life.

Where she goes. Who she goes with. I'm her mother and I don't know anything about her. I never would have done anything like this to my parents.

But the funny thing was she was special too. Smart. Educated. Got herself through college on her own. I never thought a woman could take care of herself, support herself. But she did. She even bought her own apartment. I did see her after a while. A family occasion, I think. It wasn't easy. I didn't want anyone to notice that something was wrong. I didn't want any questions. By then I was really worried. Terrible things happen to gay people and she always took such chances.

I don't think any mother wants this for her daughter. Now I have all these worries. I still can't sleep. You want to know the worst part? I'll tell you. What if people find out? What will they think of me? I feel so ashamed. How can she live this way? I'm afraid to even picture it. When I thought about her as a—a lesbian—for a while all I thought about was, was the sex part. Two women! I couldn't get my mind off of it. I tried not to think about it. I didn't like what came into my mind. I really had to block it out. I've been afraid my whole life that something bad would happen to my children. What if something bad happens to her? I didn't want people looking at her, judging her. Pointing her out. Making fun of her. Calling her names. How can she be happy?

She tried to bring it up a couple of times, suggested that I read some book. I didn't want to read any book. I didn't want to hear about it. I didn't want to talk about it. If I don't talk about it, I don't think about it. But I couldn't stay angry. I would just forget. She was still my child. She was still the same person. I mean it seemed like she was still the same person. I thought maybe she would change, meet someone. A man, of course. That's what I kept hoping. Meanwhile she had met a woman and was in a relationship. They call them partners. After a while, I would catch myself laughing at something she said. And then it would seem like old times. That what she told me wasn't real. My life has been hard enough. I wish she never told me. I wish she never said anything. I'm old. I'm not well. I want a peaceful life. This doesn't exactly leave me in peace. It's been almost five years and I still don't know what it'll take for me to be okay about this. I don't get over things that easy. We don't see much of each other now. Maybe I should try PFLAG again. I know I need to do something. I miss her. I miss the old times.

Hannah, age seventy-five and a widow, had immigrated to America from Poland as an adolescent. She grew up in the Bronx and worked briefly as a salesperson before marrying. Hannah had four children. Her daughter Sharon told her that she was a lesbian at age thirty-five in 1985. Hannah lived in Massachusetts and was interviewed in 1990.

2
Edie

I HATE MYSELF FOR HOW I BEHAVED

I HAVE TWO DAUGHTERS SEVENTEEN MONTHS APART. Carla, the lesbian daughter, had more dates in high school than my other daughter who is straight. She was very feminine looking so we had absolutely no clue, whatsoever. She was very sociable. She had boyfriends. Then she went away to college and my husband and I never heard anything about boys. She never brought any home and we began to wonder, but figured that maybe she was going out with someone that she knew we wouldn't approve of. We wondered why she wasn't saying anything, but then again, our family never talked that much about personal things. I wasn't that kind of mother. We're talking thirteen years ago. Maybe 1987. Back then parents didn't have a clue.

When we went up to her college for parents' weekends or stuff, there were nice girls around, but there weren't any boys. This persisted all through college. Then she went to graduate school and one summer, I found a letter. A love letter written by a girl and I confronted her. That's when it came pouring out and she had hidden it from us for all those years since high school. She said that it was when she got to college that she realized that she had these feelings toward other women. But she was afraid because we'd been the perfect family with perfect children and we expected only perfect things from our kids. She was right. I thought I was going to be Supermom and I was going to have these perfect children. And they were.

So she was afraid that she would disappoint us terribly and we would reject her. Apparently with her group of friends at college and graduate school, it was a very common story that their parents rejected them or wouldn't talk about it. So I was just devastated. My husband said that if that's how she was, he still loved her and accepted her and everything was fine. My husband is a doctor so if it's something that's not life threatening and terrible and this is the way it is, well, it's just let's get on with it.

But for me, it was really very, very hard. I just cried all the time and I guess I had a depression over it. It was like, how could this happen? I didn't know what I did wrong. She never played with Barbies. But I personally hated Barbies. But she never was a tomboy and she had all these boyfriends. I tried to reason it all out. I thought it was just a phase. Maybe there just weren't enough available men that she could meet. So I actually called up a dating service. I paid one hundred dollars for the dating service and I sent her picture and all this information about her. So when the dating service called her, she called me up and she said, "Mom, please don't do this." And I said, "Just try. Maybe it's just because there's not enough men around." It was then that I realized that I was really nutso.

It was devastating because I knew it was a life that would be very hard, almost impossible. The gay people I knew had very difficult lives. They were discriminated against and had a lot of difficulties and led very dangerous lives. Never having the joy of having kids or having the white wedding gown and the other part was, how was I going to tell people? What would people think of me? That I've not been a good mother? How could this happen? There is not one gay person in our family that I know of. I just couldn't stop crying.

My other kids were away at college and I called them both and told them. I called them because I thought they could change her. They'll tell her she's nuts or something. Nobody had any idea because it was so well hidden. She never displayed any tendency. Maybe if she was our age, maybe she would have gotten married years ago and tried to fight it or change, or whatever. But in her college, there was a gay and lesbian group. And in retrospect, there was this friend who went up to college with her. I never suspected she was gay. But she was and so it must have been that there was a relationship between the two of them which didn't last. So maybe in high school, they were both fighting it. Now in high school, it's "I'm gay. I'm queer. I'm here. So get used to it." I don't even know what queer means. That's the phenomenon now. Because high schools are more receptive to gay and lesbian kids.

Then I found out about PFLAG and I went right away. I cried the entire time. Buckets and buckets. I couldn't say anything. I couldn't even say my name. But I met gay and lesbian people there and they told me I was going to be all right. But I realized that I needed more help. I was just a mess. I was a wreck and I went to see a psychiatrist. She explained to me the mourning process which made sense to me. That it was the death of my daughter even though she's the same person and I had to go through that whole process of mourning in order to reach acceptance. It never affected my relationship with my husband. He was most helpful and said, "Get all the help that you need. You'll get through it. You'll work it through. It's not muscular dystrophy. It's not cancer."

I saw the psychiatrist for three months and Carla was very angry that I couldn't just accept it. But it was about the time where a lot of my friends' kids were getting married and it was really awful for me to go to these weddings. Really difficult. I kept telling Carla that I was trying. That I needed time. The hardest thing is, if I think back to thirteen years ago, I probably would have wished Carla not to be alive rather than to be gay. Selfish. It was that intense. It was that bad.

Also, I had a sister-in-law who I can't really stand and she would constantly ask me if she could fix Carla up. Finally I just blurted out that Carla was gay so just don't talk about fixing her up anymore. Instead of saying something positive to me, she told me not to tell my mother-in-law because it would kill her. But my mother-in-law died anyway without finding out. Telling other people is always ongoing and it's always difficult. Some people make it very easy, but some people are just inappropriate. Oh, you know. Ask about what happens when Carla and her partner come up and sleep in the same bed. Someone else had a baby that was born without any toes. And the guy said that he would rather have a kid born without any toes than have a gay kid. That's what he said right in front of us. This was just last year. It bothered me very much because I knew that he really meant it.

Then my other daughter got married and my son got married and I felt that they'll have children and I'll have grandchildren. So I'm lucky because a lot of people at PFLAG have just the one gay child. That was five years after Carla came out so it took me that long. Carla is not going to have kids. She definitely doesn't want children. I'm not sure that I approve of her choices of partners. The partner that she's with now, well it seems like a good partnership for her, but it's a woman who is seventeen years older than she and that disturbs me. The same as it would have been in a heterosexual relationship. This woman could have been her mother so the disturbing element for me is her age. Her partner and I get along, but I wish it would have been with someone younger and someone less controlling.

So the issue is not gay or straight. It's the person. I was very upset when they bought a house together because I always hoped maybe they would break up. It's hard for me, but this woman is a much better partner than her last partner who was a real butch lady. Not college educated. Carla's partner is not feminine, but she's not as butch. One mother at PFLAG has a daughter whose partner looks just like a man. So who can say what it is that attracts one person to another. But what happens ten years down the line, or when Carla's fifty and her partner's almost seventy? That's what I have a problem with. Her being with this gray-haired lady. But I guess they love each other and it's a fulfilling relationship. Another big negative is that my daughter doesn't have any non-gay friends. They're all gay. She has her work people. She has her family and then she has this enormous group of gay lesbian friends. When we go to her house for holidays, there's not going to be any straight people there except for us.

We had a family picture taken of my son and his wife, my daughter and my son-in-law, and Carla and her partner. When we show it to people in our family, no one knows what to say. They don't say anything. So that is more disturbing to us than anything. I'm asked about my grandchildren and my other children. But they never ask about Carla. Never. That's our family. They don't ask. It is heartbreaking. Now I just bring it up that Carla's doing really, really well. That she just got this wonderful new job and that we were on vacation with her and her partner. God damn it! I'm going to say it! I'm going to say, "Don't you dare forget her! Don't you dare!" It takes a lot of emotional strength to be able to do that. A lot of people I thought were my friends weren't strong enough or good enough to be my friends because they didn't understand or care to understand that I had a lesbian daughter. I didn't want to be pitied. It's so like I had someone with cancer. That's where society is at and people are very uncomfortable. I'd rather be alone or just have one or two friends who are able to ask about all my children.

I've been at PFLAG thirteen years. I never left. That's what helped me the most. I will still go as long as I'm healthy. To try to be a help the way I was helped. But most people now, they come once or twice. They take from it what they need, but they give nothing back. They don't come to help others. I'm not condemning them for it. I think it's the part of the society in which we live now—the "me" generation. Thirteen years ago, maybe more people had a more charitable outlook. Now children come. A lot of minority kids who have not told their parents yet. Some try and give their parents PFLAG booklets, but we can't seem to get minority parents to come. So in spite of everything, I've become an activist. I proposed a course on gays and lesbians for our town's adult education program and I've lobbied in Albany to get a hate crimes bill. But I still feel sad about Carla being gay to this day. And I think I always will.

My kids were wonderful kids. Helpful and decent and good to each other and very close. That's why they accepted Carla. None of us really believed in organized religion which probably was helpful. PFLAG has a lot of problems with very religious Catholics who come, and religious Jews too. Fathers of gay sons seem to have an impossible time with men having sex together. Especially anal sex. The men who talk about this at PFLAG feel terribly threatened and they really reject their boys. I mean parents' feelings about specific sexual acts. Like there is something about gay men's sex acts. They can't get past that picture in their mind. Like it's disgusting and perverted and biblical. Like, "Thou shall not lie with a man as with a woman." That's why God destroyed Sodom and Gomorra. I think maybe the idea of anal sex is like being treated like a woman. It's always the macho guy who is the inserter and the feminine guy who is the recipient. That's why a lot of macho men who have anal intercourse with effeminate men don't consider themselves gay. There's not so much feelings about daughters and sex. People are much freer about oral sex. It's not as Victorian as it used to be.

But AIDS is always present. PFLAG mothers will say, "You're lucky you have a lesbian daughter. I have a gay son and I think about AIDS every minute." If her son calls up and says he has a cold, she thinks he has AIDS. She knows he's not having protected sex. She just knows because gay kids think it's not going to happen to them. Or those kids feel there will be a vaccine. So unprotected sex, statistically, is on the rise. Violence too seems to be more directed towards gay men. One mother had a gay son who was beaten up and had a dreadful time in high school. Having a gay child in high school when they're still living at home is totally different. Like you know they are going out at night to God knows what gay bar, or they have a false ID, or they're bringing a boyfriend or girlfriend in the house.

I've accepted Carla being gay. She couldn't have been any other way. This is Carla. I think the thing that affected me in the beginning was that she was the daughter I was closest to. I don't know how many mothers have this favorite child. I know you shouldn't feel this, but I do and I feel guilty. I've tried to let her know that I love her unconditionally and that I'm there for her. I've apologized and told her that I'm very sorry that I couldn't handle it better. I hate myself for how I behaved.

Edie, age sixty-six, was married and had worked as a nurse. She identified as Catholic and had three children. Her daughter Carla told her that she was a lesbian at age twenty-three in 1987. Edie was an active member of PFLAG—helping other parents to adjust to a lesbian daughter or gay son—as well as a LGBT activist. Her other political interests were civil rights and the fair housing movement. Edie lived in Westchester County, New York and was interviewed in 2000.

3

Sara

SHE WASN'T GOING TO BE THE NICE LITTLE LESBIAN I HAD HOPED SHE WOULD BE

OUR DAUGHTER JANE IS NOW JAIME. But first she was a lesbian and was sixteen when she first came out. My husband and I, we were devastated. We cried all night and spent hours worrying about her future, how other people would treat her, how it would affect her life, her career plans. We had very little knowledge about what it meant to be gay. We struggled with it for weeks. She tried to reassure us, saying that she was happy and felt so free now that she had come out to us. We even went to PFLAG at her insistence although we thought that it was she that needed to be there. We also joined a political action group that defended the civil rights of gays because we felt that she needed to have some role models in the gay community and meet other gay people her age.

Then she went off to college and our dreams were completely dashed within a semester. She had gone off full of hope and excitement, but within a few weeks she was concerned that one of her roommates knew she was gay and didn't want to be in the same room with her. So she would stay out of the room. Then we learned that she was staying in bed all day and hadn't gone to class for most of the semester. When we confronted her, she fell apart and began to act very distant and out of character. I was getting pretty fed up with her, but at the same time I loved her to a point that she was driving me to distraction. In any case, she dropped out of college, moved in with her girlfriend, and began to work full time.

It was immediately apparent that all her friends were gay and butch. There were so many shaved heads and she had a crew cut. I kept hoping this was a gay pride sort of thing and that she would modify after a few years and that she was just sowing her oats. But she did seem fairly happy. Then she moved back in with us along with her girlfriend. While they were living here, I noticed a book called, *Body Alchemy* lying around. When I looked at it, I could feel my whole body bracing. It was full of very masculine women and pictures that I couldn't stand looking at. I was pretty horrified. I used to talk about this time as the death of dreams because, one by one, they were going down the drain and I had to face the fact that she wasn't going to be the nice little lesbian I had hoped she would be.

I talked to her about it and she was pretty defensive and I felt very defensive and angry too. Then she and her girlfriend moved out and things lightened up because we didn't have to confront her on a daily basis. My other daughters kept reassuring me that she was just going through late adolescence and would probably come around eventually. But I think I knew in my heart that this just wasn't the case. Several tattoos later, she informed me that she had changed her name legally to Jaime. That in itself really upset me and my husband and I still have trouble remembering, even now, not to say Jane. She was very belligerent over my forgetting in the beginning and for about six to eight months I was happy to avoid her as much as I could and to put my head in the sand.

The word "trans man" hadn't come up yet and when it did, it was a confirmation of our very worst fears. At one point, she told me she would be taking male hormones and beginning her transition. I felt like I had walked off the end of a dock and fallen into muddy waters and that I was unable to get back onto that dock. By then I was on anti-depressants and even they didn't really help. I went through a very dark period for a few months, wanting to avoid friends and just wanting to just disappear. I finally realized that I was not helping myself and I found an online support group called Transfamilies of Cleveland. I e-mailed and got in touch with other mothers of female-to-male children and chose to write to three of them who had children in the same age group. That changed our lives. I felt so connected to other people who were undergoing the same experience and all of them seemed to be as shocked and stunned that this was happening to them as I was.

At first, I had sworn I would not contribute one penny to Jaime's transition. But in the end I decided to offer to pay for the top surgery that he was wanting because I thought that getting this done might enable him to get on with his life. After the surgery, when I looked at Jaime, I realized how much he had changed. My child is transgendered and nothing was going to turn him back into my little girl. He had bulked up with testosterone and didn't even look like my Jane anymore and I could accept that without crying for probably the first time. When I looked at him, I now thought of him as a *he*.

It didn't affect my relationship with my husband. It was a crisis for us to weather together. But my other children thought it was a phase and that Jaime would outgrow it. When he had his surgery, they were very shocked. They didn't know whether to call her *he* or my brother so it did affect our family relationships. One daughter was very angry that I paid for the surgery and facilitated it happening. The others stay in touch and go out with her and her girlfriend all the time, but they just don't talk about it. But although we were still really suffering, both my husband and I felt a need to be supportive. I definitely felt that he and I needed to be the ones that set the tone for the family to follow. It was difficult, but we knew we would get through it as a family. My relationship with Jaime improved quickly and we have gotten closer after she transitioned and had the surgery and went trans. It was then I felt an acceptance and at peace with this that I hadn't felt up to this point and was much more able to be a real support to him.

But it has greatly affected our friendships and extended family relationships. I feel animosity towards many family members on my husband's side who have not been able to say anything much more than they wish us luck, but they know that this is not what God wanted for Jane to be doing. Our friendships? Well when Jane came out as gay, we sorted through our friendships and people who could not deal with it, or who were uncomfortable with it. We either brought them along and helped educate them to the point where they did much better or we just didn't see much of them. I don't think my husband has told anyone at work.

If she told me as a child, I don't think I could have coped. I really think I would have fallen apart. I would have taken her to a psychiatrist. I would have just not believed it. I read on the Transfamily Support Line that many more parents now have children who believe they're transgender and these children are five, six, seven years old. I am so amazed at how well these parents do with regard to dealing with children and letting them express themselves. I don't think I would have been that good a parent. I wish I could say I would, but I wouldn't have. I'm also so very thankful my daughter came out as a lesbian before she became transgendered because it gave me a chance to grow and to take the step out beyond, to let go, and to learn that I can't control my children's destinies.

I have always loved this child and this child has been my heart. She, he is still my heart. Nothing has changed. I have gained a great deal of appreciation for the way my daughter handled this for the most part, and the way she's handling it now that she's gained some maturity. When she was a lesbian, I thought her life would be fine. I had adjusted to that. She had a wonderful girlfriend. I thought that she would have a wonderful community. I think he'll be happy now, but I think he will have feelings of great loss. In talking to other female-to-males, they miss their community of dykes. They miss being part of a community and they are somewhat not accepted in all sorts of groups where they used to be accepted. Jaime lives in a very gay area so it's very hard to stand out. There's so many odd people living there. But the thing I most would like to know is that they are accepted and that they can move into the world and be safe. My greatest fear is that my child might be discovered by somebody who would be angry as in the case of Teena Brandon. Somebody who would harm her, or him, physically.

Jaime's in a relationship with a lesbian woman. They've been together three years now. We love her and one of the things that frightened us was that she might not be able to go through this process of his transitioning. I'd say Jaime is actually a straight male now. My feelings about this? Confusion. But if it works for them, that's what I care about. They're a wonderful couple, very caring about each other. His life has changed too in that he has a full-time job and it's very demanding and he has a lot of responsibility. So that part of his life has changed and he seems to like being part of the trans community, attending seminars and things like that.

I was raised in a proper Canadian household. It was be seen and not heard. Children were to be perfect, but my mother was a wonderful mother. I was an adopted only child so she was very happy to have a child. But my mother was a very, very exacting mother. She was a perfectionist. On the other hand, she wanted everything to be just right for me. She wanted my life to be good. She wanted me to be a good person and she wanted to do the best for me. So, I don't really wish anything different. I'm very grateful for the mother I had. But I don't think I was the best mother when my children were younger. I was too demanding. But as our children have grown and forced us to come along with them, I've learned a lot. I think my strength now is that I can be supportive through most anything and I have learned to listen to my children. I wish I could have worried less about teaching them to do everything properly and taught them to be a little freer and to listen to their own voices.

I've learned that there are people who will always think it's wrong and they will always make comments or feel sorry for us. I have learned to deflect what they say and turn it around into something positive and the most problems I've had are with people who are with the Christian Right. But I have found a way that I can talk to them and tell them what I think they need to know about it. And at the same time, let them see that there is a commonality. That this is my child. I love my child and that we're all God's children whether we are trans or gay or straight and that I'm sure that we can agree that God meant us to love our children. And then I move on.

Parents that can't accept, I think are living in a very rigid box. I feel that they allow themselves to be ruled by fear and denial and they allow their faith, in most cases, to dictate to them exactly how they will think on this particular subject. I think they have to be willing to take a risk and to step out and get out of the box, and that is not an easy thing for any of us. I don't feel animosity towards them, but I feel sadness for them because they are missing out on their child's life. I feel particularly sad for children who lose their parents in cases like that and feel like they don't have a family anymore.

I can't imagine anything worse than that. I just can't imagine how a parent could shut their mind down to a child just because of their sexual orientation. When my daughter came out, that was never a question. My husband and I never ever thought of not having a relationship with her because she was a lesbian, or not accepting who she was. She is our daughter and, you know, she was a wonderful daughter. She's a wonderful son now. We've learned the important thing is that we love our child and I have trouble dealing with parents who just can't take that step. In PFLAG, I try very hard to help them get over the hump so they can accept their child for who they are because I think that's so important. This is your child. There's nothing that can separate you from your child unless you choose to do so.

When I began to talk more to Jaime about his transition and in talking to other parents and to the trans people I met online, I began to see how courageous they were and developed an interest in and a respect for them. Jaime also introduced us to many trans people and I began to see them as pioneers and as people who are incredibly brave and self-knowledgeable. I realized they were just like everyone else and was just totally amazed that these people could go through the incredible rejection and changes that they have to go through in order to be true to themselves and to be who they are. I am now co-chair of our local PFLAG chapter and I want to do everything possible to make Jaime's life and the life of all the people we've met through him equal and have the civil rights of straight people. I know that transgender completely baffles people who don't have any knowledge of it and they think of it in terms of weird, kinky, or freaky unless they are educated on the subject. Transgendered people are people just like everyone else.

I've come to understand transgender to be an inner longing to be another gender, not the gender they were born with. I believe that it is something biological or genetic. I believe that it is something chemical in the brain or in the hormonal wash of the fetus. I've grown a tremendous amount from this experience and I'm very grateful for Jaime. Now my husband and I want to do everything possible to make Jaime's life, and the life of all the people we've met through him, equal in life and civil rights to straight people. I have a very strong belief in God and believe that has helped me to go through this a great deal. I believe that God wanted Jaime to be the way Jaime is, and that he is being true to himself. I value that. I've learned to accept that I couldn't determine everything about my child.

At this stage, I have the great reward of being forced to grow at age fifty-seven and not be sitting around and worrying about a bridge club, or the height of my heels or the color of my hair. To be given the opportunity to really learn and grow and to be part of this child's life. Still there are times when I have trouble with pronouns and think of Jaime as my daughter. Like his sisters. Like one of my girls. But sometimes I wonder if I will ever see him as my son or if I will always see him as Jane who wants to be Jaime and so we go along with it.

Sara, age fifty-seven, was born in Canada. She was married, attended two years of college, and had worked in real estate. Of Sara's six children, one daughter identified as a lesbian and a second daughter, Jane—now Jaime—came out as a lesbian when she was sixteen and then as transgender five years later in 1998. Although Sara's husband was a Methodist chaplain, she did not identify with any Protestant denomination. She was supportive of progressive and social justice causes including feminism, civil rights, the environment and peace movement, and was active in PFLAG and the transgender rights movement. Sara lived in Washington State and was interviewed by mail in 2001.

4

Karen

GAY WAS A PIECE OF CAKE

WHEN DONNY TOLD ME SHE WAS GAY, she was probably around sixteen. I was suspicious. A combination of behavior, appearance, working out all the time. She was really very unhappy from an early age and obviously her sexual preference didn't help. My ex-husband and I knew that she needed some kind of therapy. She didn't have friends. She wasn't doing well in school. So she went before she came out. I don't know if it helped. I don't know what she told the therapist, or didn't tell the therapist.

When I found out, I thought, "Okay, we're not gonna go down the aisle with the dress and the boyfriend." I was disappointed. Sad for just those reasons. Wedding. Grandchildren. The things I was not gonna have as a mother. In those days, it was unusual for a lesbian couple to have a baby. But on the other hand, I thought there's nothing I can do about it. I knew that I wasn't going to ask if she was sure. I was educated enough to know this wasn't a stage she was going through. I knew she came this way. I did have a gay uncle and interestingly enough, even before I had children, I always read about homosexuals. It fascinated me. Absolutely fascinated me as to what would make somebody be this. My friends used to tease me all the time.

My ex-husband was okay with it. To him, it was as long as you're happy. He didn't wring his hands over it and he wasn't surprised either. Donny was always on the butchy side. It was hard on his younger brother. You have to understand this is the football-playing, varsity football, lacrosse-playing brother who was very jock, rah-rah high school and had all these friends and was the captain of the team. Everybody would come over and they all knew he had a sister. He was at a very bad age for a boy to find out. He's also not one of those in touch with your feelings kind of guy, as far as I know him. He just didn't tell anyone. But you know everyone figured it out. When everyone stops asking if your daughter or sister has a boyfriend, you know that they know. Because when you get together with people, that's all they ask. "How is your child? Does she have a boyfriend? Does he have a girlfriend?" When they stopped asking, I knew that they figured it out. Without me sitting down and saying, "Gee, by the way, Donny is gay or Donny is transgendered."

I knew when he told me. Otherwise, I had no clue. I didn't see him that often. But I did notice that every time I saw him, he was starting to look butchier and butchier as a gay girl. Body language, dress, manner of speech, manner of walking. Almost like he was over-trying, trying too hard. Overstating it. I said to myself, "My God, we're getting butchier and butchier." She had girlfriends. One or two would come and stay. I had no problem with that. They weren't very feminine. They weren't very butchy. They were just regular. But the thing that amazed me was the kind of girl he always was attracted to. Never Jewish girls. I would say jokingly before he transgendered, "Couldn't you at least bring home some nice Jewish gay girl?" I really didn't care. It really didn't matter to me. I was just curious. Teasing. You know how Jewish mothers are always teasing their children to get somebody Jewish.

I don't remember exactly what he said when she told me. I mean he tried to explain it to me because I never heard of it. Never ever heard of it. I knew transvestite, but I never heard of transgendered. It was a shock. "You're what! You're not really a she? You're a he! What happened? How could that happen?" I know she must have been born that way, but I needed to understand where it came from. Why this happens. How somebody is like that.

She gave me things to read that were helpful because I had no information. She sent me stuff from PFLAG and chat lines so I could chat with a couple of other mothers. I had thought gay was a piece of cake. It was really nothing for me as a parent. But this was now an outward thing. This was now a physical change. Operation, hormones, voice change, hair change. This now is not my child. Who was I going to talk to? I went to a therapist. I knew I needed help. But this therapist was not particularly well versed and she gave me advice about accepting things and figuring things out. But nothing about transgender. She really didn't understand at all.

I didn't see him for a while when he was taking hormones. That's when a lot of the changes happened. Then he came into the city to see his father and I was planning to go in as well when my ex-husband called me up and said, "I'm just telling you, you're not going to be very happy with what you see. It's not going to be easy and I thought it was my place to let you know so that you're not shocked when you walk in the door. Because that's the last thing you want to be is shocked." He was right. I was shocked. I had left really a girl, a gay girl, and now I have somebody with some facial hair and a big neck. It was a shock. But, after a while, you know, it's still your child. You get over what the outward appearance is and it just becomes your child again. It's the same person in a different shape. Now when I see him, the changes aren't much. It was just that initial shock. It was the same person. It was my child. It's the same Danielle that I knew when she was six or seven except she's a he and her name is Donny. I just gradually accepted it. I kind of learned all about it so it helped me to let it go.

I wasn't sad or depressed. I was troubled. I got past that and then it basically resolved. You know what? The thing that made it easier is that Donny has never been happier as a person. It's almost like that all these years, this is really what he needed to do to be happy. And to me, as I get older and have been through my share, if you can be happy, you've accomplished something. Because it's not easy to be happy. I have friends who are gay or in lesbian marriages or relationships who are fourteen times happier than half of the heterosexual relationships or marriages of people that I know. So to me, if you're happy, fine. That's how I am. Glad you're happy. And he's very happy. He's had a new girlfriend for a while. Happy as can be.

My ex-husband had moved away after we separated and it was much easier for him. He's not friendly with people here anymore and he has all new friends and those people don't really know he had a daughter. Where I live, I have eighteen-year-old relationships. All the people whose kids my own kids grew up with, they all knew I had a daughter and a son. I gradually told them one by one, but I actually haven't told that many. It's not that easy for me to tell them that Donny is a he. But I found that after I told a few people, it became easier. It was the barrage of questions and the "Oh my God!" kind of thing that I expected. I wasn't comfortable saying it. It's me who didn't want to go through the whole conversation.

It took me a year to accept this. I mean, I didn't get up in the morning and say, "Okay, well my child's transgender and it's all right." I was in horror at first. I didn't tell anybody, nobody. Not a living soul. Because I couldn't deal with it. I just couldn't deal with it. "What are you talking about? How could you do that? What do you mean you're going to be a he?" I didn't say that to him. This is my own dialogue. I'm thinking, "How am I going to tell anybody? They're not going to understand. I don't understand." Not ashamed. More shocked and asking myself how do I sit down and tell this to somebody. I just found it so difficult.

My son was tough. But he had no right to just write this person off like they were dead because he couldn't accept it. He's twenty-three years old. How would you feel if you had enough trouble getting through life and your own sibling wouldn't even accept you? So maybe that he's becoming a little older and out in the world and out of his college fraternity, he'll come around and he has been better about it. My boyfriend didn't know Donny as a girl. He only knows him as an almost him. He said to me, "I don't have anything to compare it to. You can show me a picture, but I never knew him any other way." Interestingly enough, I went and told my father. This was a hard thing for me to do. He's ninety years old. To tell him that his granddaughter is not a granddaughter, but is a grandson. How is a ninety year-old man going to understand this? I guess then was the time to tell everybody in the family. That's what Donny wanted. He wanted to be accepted and be part of the family.

I actually went to therapy to help me do this. How do I tell this old man? How is he going to understand this? I had enough trouble understanding it. My therapist said that I'd be surprised. Old people do a lot better than you think. My father's also very alert and very up on stuff and is a very wonderful human being. But even so, how was I going to tell him? What do I say? "Dad, sit down. Guess what?" But my father said to me, "I feel so sorry for her. How horrible it must have been wanting to be one thing and to be something else." I looked at him and I went, "Oh my God, I can't believe it! You did better than I did." So then my father proceeds to tell me about five generations in the family tree who were gay or lesbian. This one's daughter. This great uncle. I called Donny up and told him and he was fascinated with it. Well, I guess Donny just took it to the next level and totally changed as opposed to being just gay.

I was really basically a stay-at-home mother for thirteen years because I didn't work. I was medium permissive, not horribly permissive, and not horribly strict. There were certain things I didn't care about like how much television you watched. How many cookies you ate. That kind of stuff never bothered me. For grades and stuff, I just said you just have to do fine. It wasn't that you had to get an "A" or that kind of thing. Maybe my field helped. Dealing with children with problems, with disabilities. Seeing all kinds of things that can go awry. And I think, having been divorced and having to pick myself up and totally change my life. Everything like house, life, family. All kinds of stuff. And having to go through some adversity myself and seeing that you can do more than you think you can do. I think that helped too and also, as I said, I'm so big on whatever makes you happy. It's so hard to be happy. And it's been so hard for Donny to be happy, that if he's finally happy, I'm happy. That's really all a mother wants is for her children to be happy. I mean me. I was never one that you had to go to this school or that school. I never did that because I know plenty of people who went to fabulous schools and are miserable.

My mother is not alive. She knew nothing of anything having to do with Donny except that Donny was a granddaughter. My mother would not have accepted this. My father is an easier person to get along with. A more understanding, non-judgmental person. My mother was extremely judgmental, critical, and insecure. So therefore, everything on the outside had to be very bright if you're not secure enough in yourself. She didn't have one of the ideal growing up lives either. I think that she was a very insecure person who was a very good mother and worked very hard to be a good mother and she really loved her children. But she was very overbearing, over-protective, over-burdening, and very much embarrassed if you did not look and follow exactly how everybody else looked—because she felt it was a reflection on how you were brought up. She wasn't happy that Donny wasn't one of those little preppy girls with the nail polish and the lipstick. She always used to say, "How come you don't have any nail polish on? How come you don't have any lipstick?" And Donny would say, "I just don't wear it."

I don't know how someone would know. I know that Donny knew for a very long time. From the time she was—he was—young, he knew that he was certainly gay. That he didn't like boys like girls liked boys. Then as I watched, there became a gradual butchiness. A continuum. That's how I call it. We start out born a girl like everyone else. A girl, a baby girl, and then gradually a manliness, a masculineness comes out. Now we say we're gay and we're still walking on that continuum. We're still becoming more and more masculine until the end result is we've changed. How we know that inside, how he knew that, I have no clue. I never asked that question. Never occurred to me to ask it. It's like, like this is something that I needed to do. I really was a boy. I just was born a girl. I really was a boy in a girl's body. So he was feeling that he was a boy, but outside he wasn't a boy. I said, "Donny, you've now hit it! You changed sex! That's it! There's nowhere left on the continuum for you to go. What's left, Donny? Is there something I'm missing? What other shocker can you give me?" But he made it, so now he's outside a boy and happy. Just that we're short. We're a short boy. But we were short for a girl. So now he's an even shorter boy. He's not real happy about that.

Time is a big healer. Well, it is a process. Do I call her him? This is only a year old pronoun. A year and a half old. It's a habit. Her father? No, I mean his father. His father has the same problem too. He. She. It's easier if you use Donny. This way it's okay, especially in front of Donny who doesn't like it if you mess up the pronouns. So sometimes he's a he. But only a he. I can't think of him as a son. He's not a son. It's too extreme. If people ask me, I have to really stop and say I have two sons. But if I don't think, I'll just say I have a son and a daughter.

I took all of the pictures out of the house of Donny as a she. There weren't that many. He asked me to when he came to visit. Oh, I have them, but I put them away. I think he felt I didn't accept it if those pictures were still there. I put a picture up of Donny as Donny. I have pictures of Donny getting butchier and butchier. So I think I could make a kind of a sequence. There's a picture when Donny was thirteen with the long curly hair. The gorgeous hair, big billows of hair. From there to wearing her hair pulled back. I guess severe to look like a boy. Pulling her hair back, then cutting it short, a dress which he was forced to wear. Then corduroys hanging down and the big flannel shirts when he was still a girl.

I haven't had a daughter for so long that I didn't even think about it because he never was daughtery. Dresses, makeup. Maybe I initially missed having a daughter, but it's been so long ago. If I would get make-up samples, I would give them to my son to give to his girlfriend, or a girl that he knew because Donny would never have any part of any of it. So I sort of haven't had a daughter even though she was a girl. I had a masculine daughter. It made it easier. We didn't go from makeup and dresses to being this. We were sort of on the way in a slow process. If I took this varsity football jock son and all of a sudden he came home and told me that he was a girl, that would really be more of a shock.

To Donny's credit, he did this whole transgender change by himself. Without me. In other words, without parental help. Very self-reliant and very able to handle everything. I offered to come down when he had the breast removal surgery because this is not a piece of cake. But Donny told me he didn't want me to. That he would be fine and such and such a person was going to take care of him. I admire the self-reliance. He's the same person, but happier. Less hard. Less hostile. There was always somewhat of a hard edge. I think he was just miserable. I really do. I think my father was one hundred percent right. How horrible it must have been.

I'd say we're closer now. Donny is not one to call me up. I mean, it can be two, three weeks. If I don't call, he doesn't call. He's busy with his own life and I'm not on his "I'm going to call my mother list or my father list." We really aren't alone in that respect. They're not one of those kids. Neither one of my kids. You know how some kids will call their mothers everyday. We just never had that for whatever reason. But he'll talk to me more now about life and what's going on and relationships. I think we have a better relationship now that he's more of an adult and settled in his life and knows that I accept it. It seems easier now to be chattier.

I think Donny had a perception of me as me being disappointed in her or him as a child because she was not the daughter that I expected. I think, sure I must have gone through that period of saying, "Whoa, I don't have the daughter that I expected to have with the ribbons and the bows and the you like to dress up and everything." I told Donny that I was sorry. I'm sure that it was true and I'm sorry that came across. Obviously, I didn't want it to, but you learn that kids are smarter than you think they are. They pick up on more. I think Donny maybe was disappointed he wasn't or she wasn't what I wanted. I do think he's appreciative of me being accepting of him. It took a while for me to be understanding, but now I do think Donny is very appreciative of how interested I am in it and how good and accepting I am.

I don't understand parents who stop seeing their children. I can't see how anybody could do that. I have friends from way back whose parents stopped talking to them because they married out of their religion. I thought that was the stupidest thing I ever heard of. Who cares? I think it's deplorable. I think that some parents are in total denial and they can't deal with it and won't deal with it, so this way they don't have to deal with it. They just shut it down, shut it off, put it away, compartmentalize it, get rid of it. They don't have a child anymore and don't have to deal with it and that's easier for them. I think it's the weaker ones who just shut it down. I think it's harder to deal with it rather than just shut it down.

I have concerns. I think he frequented a very underground world for a while as a gay girl. Lots of unusual clubs. I certainly think he lives not in the best areas because he can't afford to live anywhere else. I'm never happy where he lives. But it doesn't seem to bother him. Now, it could be my little, as Donny likes to say, suburbanite personality projecting here. But I think it's more of a hope that he knows what he's doing. I don't really know much about Donny's daily life. Except he always has a girlfriend. Maybe that's because of having a grownup child—or maybe because of having a gay or a transgender child. Or maybe it's just Donny. I do wonder about some things like sex. Like what does he do and how does he do it, have sex. But I would never ask. I mean, after all, I am his mother.

Karen, age fifty-four, worked as a special education teacher. She was divorced and had plans to re-marry. She had two children and although identified as Jewish, stated she was not religious. Her child, Danielle—now Donny—disclosed as a lesbian at age sixteen and then as transgender at age twenty-five in 1998. Karen was supportive of progressive and social justice causes including feminism, civil rights, and the peace movement. She lived in West-chester County, New York and was interviewed in 2001.

5

Anna

WHY WOULD YOU WANT TO BE A WHITE MALE?

WHEN MY DAUGHTER, MARLA, WAS A TEENAGER, she was a very spirited, quite stubborn and, at times, very challenging young person. Full of opinions and ideas and a lot of pretty serious risk-taking behaviors. We've always had a very close relationship, but at times fraught with difficulties. She had lots of political opinions and was very feisty and, at a fairly young age, had an incredible social conscience and awareness of injustices. She became very active in the environmental movement and, of course, in her own true fashion, she protested and got arrested. We were there with her every day through the court trial. But I knew always that she was very committed to whatever she stood up for and that what we had to do, as parents, was to try and be as calm as possible. At the same time, I've always been very proud of her commitment and willingness to take on lots of issues and social struggles.

Then, in her early twenties, it was fairly obvious to us that maybe she was unsure about her own sexuality and that she was a lesbian or bisexual—or maybe wasn't one hundred percent clear exactly what her preference was. But none of that seemed to be too challenging for us. Some of our women friends were lesbians and we had several male friends who were very out and open about being gay. So when she told us that she was a lesbian, it didn't really come as a surprise to us although she was kind of flitting back and forth between having relationships with women and men. But they all seemed to be very difficult with lots of ups and downs which kind of mirrored how she was going through life at that period of time.

Then she told us, my husband and I—this was almost five years ago—that she wanted to talk to us about a decision that she had made. She probably had agonized over when to tell us for quite a long time. She told us that she was transgendered and it was the first time that she had openly said it in such a very blunt way. But it shouldn't have been as much of a surprise as it was because she had written a paper where she referred to herself as a transgendered person. But I can honestly say that I didn't understand what that meant. She just looked very butch, but that was fairly common for lots of young women in terms of style so she wasn't really that dramatically different. But when I look back, I think it was just one indication about this decision.

When she told us about the transgendered path she was taking, it did come as a hard thing to understand with lots and lots of emotions. I did know of a couple of people that were transgendered. They lived their lives—first as men and then went in two different directions—some as drag queens and the others as men. But I did not know anybody who was born a female and who was going to live their life as a man. So needless to say, I was in a state of shock. I didn't know what to say. If I expressed my feelings, it would have caused a whole lot of conflict, but I couldn't give my blessings because it was going to be such an uphill climb and very difficult in terms of adjustments and society's acceptance and everything else. So deep down I thought, "Here we go again. It's just one of those unexpected little paths that we're gonna have to deal with." I did wonder if there was something about my parenting or if something had happened to her in her earlier years. Typical mother's responses mixed in with guilt and wondering how we would explain this.

Typical in the way she sometimes communicated, she asked for our support and acceptance and I felt that, written between the lines, she was asking for a lot of assistance. I wasn't sure what I could do and that we were going to have to figure this out. After all, she was our daughter and while we had had lots of ups and downs, there was never ever a time when I thought that I would not be there to be supportive and to help her, no matter what. But I just never really figured that there would be a conversation like this. So there were tears and anxiety for the rest of that day. When she left, I remember feeling very emotional and wanting very much to give her lots of big hugs, but at the same time thinking, "Oh my God, what the hell is this next little while going to be like, both in her life and our life?" So needless to say, I guess I was in a state of shock. I had lots of tears and no doubt she had tears as well.

For many years we were very aware that if there were two paths to take, she always seemed to take the path that was fraught with all kinds of difficulties rather than the easy road to travel. So my immediate reaction was, as I said, "Oh, my God, here we go again!" When she was an adolescent, she really seemed to have low self-esteem and some of the friendships that she had reflected that. There were times when I knew she was drinking excessively and was probably experimenting with drugs. For sure, marijuana and she told us she had done LSD. But, thank goodness, no cocaine or heroin. I think she was really lost and was allowing herself to be quite easily manipulated. Before transitioning, there were periods in her life where she seemed to be quite depressed and had a lot of difficulty coping and this just seemed to me to be more of the same. I had hoped that as she got a little bit older, that there would be more of an even keel and that she would find herself and feel quite comfy with herself and settle down. I thought maybe this was what had been troublesome and maybe this was exactly what was going to help her calm down and find her place in life.

For me, it was just a matter of time. I started reading anything that I could get my hands on. She also provided some material for me to read and it was really just a matter of trying to get a grip on how the hell to understand and figure it out. There wasn't really much that I could do anyway, because clearly this was a decision that she had made. So I could either eat my heart out and be an obstructionist, or have a very tense relationship—or just get on with accepting it. That's what happened bit by bit.

I think that the hardest thing of all was something very simple. I couldn't get the pronouns right. She told us quite clearly that her new name was Jared, but that she had kept her original birth name as her middle name. She made it very clear that that's who she wanted to be known as, although she hadn't changed it legally yet. I did call her by her new name, but kept referring to her as her and as she and that was very difficult and awkward. She was great and kept on saying that it was okay and that we'd get it eventually. True enough, I began to pay a lot of attention to how I referred to him. But do I think of my child as a daughter, or as a son? I guess I think of him as who he is with a male name and a persona in many ways that is male. But at the same time, I don't fit him into a category necessarily. I'm just starting to refer to him as my son.

When the transition period took place, he began to look not like a female. His haircut was indeed male and there was a little bit of facial hair, but it seemed to me as though he fits somewhere in the middle. He views himself, in appearance, definitely as a male. I know that one of the most important events was the surgery to remove his breasts and that was incredibly important to his identity as a male. For me, it was fraught with fear and some confusion because we had friends who had to have mastectomies as a result of cancer. But that was a choice that Jared was making that was not at all rooted in the same symptoms and illness that go hand in hand with that kind of surgery. I was just excessively worried about whether the surgery would go well and if it would be successful.

He had the surgery and we were at the hospital making sure that everything was okay. Then he came to our house to recuperate. He had a wonderful friend who stayed here as well and who was just so kind and caring and much better at the physical things that had to be taken care of than I am. I'm just no good at being a nurse when it comes to blood and tubes, so I knew what I could do and that was make sure that everything was okay in terms of the food and everything. So it was wonderful to have that friend here. I knew too that there was no turning back and that I better come to grips with it, the sooner the better. Still I had lots and lots of concerns about my daughter and that life was going to be incredibly difficult. I wondered about work and what it meant in terms of her ability to support herself and if people would accept her or reject her, and if she would always be on the fringes. I was extremely concerned about her taking hormones.

We told some immediate family members and we did tell my father, his grandfather. For me, it was made a whole lot easier because my dad, who was eighty at the time, took it upon himself to proudly state that he had always wished that he had a grandson although he loved his four granddaughters very much—and now, lo and behold, he had one. He told a lot of his friends and cronies who had sons or daughters or grandchildren and who kept their stories in the closet if they were gay or lesbian. My father proclaimed that, unlike them, he was gonna talk about it openly and show people that there was only reasons to be proud and nothing at all to be ashamed of. The result is that Jared now feels really comfortable to be around our extended family.

We also had to work very consciously at remembering who knew and who didn't and that was always very difficult because the whole world didn't know right away. One of the hardest things was that when people who had known us for a long time, but didn't know about Jared, asked about our daughters. Sometimes I explained that we now had a daughter and a son, and that the person that they knew as Marla is now Jared and is living his life as a male. In other situations, I just don't really want to get into a discussion about it and so I just say, "Fine. Thank you very much," and move on to another topic. It's still difficult because while more and more people do know, there are equally as many people that don't, and so I feel like it's a little bit of a schizy kind of thing.

There have been a few people who have been shocked and kind of speechless, but I can honestly say that if they had really negative responses, it must have been behind my back. We've always been selective about who our friends were and who we spend time with in terms of acceptance of diversity and so we wouldn't spend any time with a bunch of rednecks or people who are racist or incredibly biased. Having grown up with some anti-Semitism in the past, we were probably prepared for homophobic comments and knew how to talk to people about our female-to-male oldest child.

My husband was much calmer in his responses. He was the calm one, the practical one and the not so emotional one, and sometimes that was a good balance for my way of coping. They had always been relatively close with each other. They would talk about ideas and their big connection was the concern around what was happening in the world and the local political scene. It was a real intellectual bond. Our younger daughter has always been a very calm and easygoing person and I think that's because she could see that there was enough stress and anxiety between us and Marla. She accepted her older sister's decision in a very matter of fact way and kind of took the approach of, "Okay, whatever." I recently learned that she has only just begun to talk about it with some of her friends.

I have an incredible belief in the importance of family and community in raising children. Both the collective and the individual kind of responsibility. I truly do believe that it takes a village to raise children and I wanted to be like every other mother I knew, the best mother possible. Do I have any particular regrets? Well, sometimes I do. Other times I'm able to laugh and not take them so seriously. It was a challenge to raise Marla from a very early age. She was so intellectually bright and well-advanced for her years. She questioned everything and every year presented some little difficulty. We gave the kids a culturally very rich upbringing and had strict values about not watching much television or eating unhealthy foods. Now they laugh at us because they used to just go across the street and eat the kind of full of sugar food that they weren't allowed to have at home. They would also watch television there and it was everything, of course, that they were not allowed to watch at home.

I think that my expectations were high in terms of independence. Her intellect confused me and, at times, I thought she was capable of more than she was emotionally. But I don't suffer a whole lot of regrets or guilt. I did the best I could and I'm sure I could have done some things differently and maybe I could have even done some things better. But I did what I knew how and the best that I could at the time. I read a lot. I participated with other moms who were raising kids and we used to talk about parenting and different approaches. But I never thought I'd be a perfect mother. It's a whole lot easier to give other people advice and really difficult to figure it all out yourself with your own kids.

I was raised as a secular Jew, a Humanist with a tremendous emphasis on Jewish culture and tradition. But absolutely no religion or spirituality whatsoever. My father and mother were strict in some ways, but incredibly loving and I was raised in an extremely warm and caring environment. We grew up also in a political environment and my mother would always remind us that we had to share what we had. But when I was a teenager, I became very angry and annoyed at her strictness and her expectations and probably was difficult. Later on, my mom and dad would joke with me when Jared had some really rough patches growing up, saying that it was payback time.

Jared is in a relationship although they don't live together. It's absolutely fascinating in terms of sexual orientation because during the first phase of transitioning, he had a girlfriend and they still live in the same house together and are incredibly good friends. We also just recently learned that this girlfriend is now in a lesbian relationship and had worked for a number of years in the sex trade. So the whole question of sexual orientation and sexuality is quite fascinating. The relationship he's in now is with another female-to-male person. I guess any stereotypes left in my brain have all been completely dismantled because I no longer predict anything at all about gender and sexual orientation when it comes to Jared. My feelings are that I just want him to find happiness in friendships and intimate relationships. It's the person that matters to me a whole lot more than the sexual orientation. I just don't really care at all as long as it's a good, healthy, kind, loving, caring relationship. That's what matters to me.

I want Marla to be able to be self-sufficient and find work that she both enjoys and that allows her to be who she is and make the kind of contribution that she wants. But he's still having some patches of depression and that concerns me. For the first couple of years on the hormones, he seemed to be on a much more even keel emotionally But since he's gone off them, he's had a bit of a rough patch and I don't know if that's hormonally related. Does he seem to be the same person as before? Yes, in some ways, but not in others. How he's different, well, I'm a bit short on words. I actually think that the way he makes some decisions and goes through life now challenges some of my own understandings around gender. In some ways he does fit some of my stereotypical images of how some men, obviously not all, do cope and it is different than women. When I think back as to how Jared played as a child, in some ways he played the way I have observed many more boys play with things. I've worked with lots and lots of kids and a lot of Jared's play was kind of mechanical and stuff like that. He never,

ever played with dolls. He never wanted stuffed animals.

At a recent trans meeting, Jared told us he wanted us to meet someone. This middle-aged woman came over and she should never have been wearing high heels because, just like me, she couldn't walk in them. I just couldn't understand why we were being introduced until it dawned on me that it was a male teacher that Marla had in high school and it turned out that he was now living his life as a woman. They were quite intrigued by having rediscovered each other. Jared was quite frustrated at that particular meeting and said that the men that live their lives now as women still behave in a group like men. It just really made me laugh when he said that as he was so used to process and consensus building because of the feminist movement so he still expects to be a part of a group that functions in that way. He said, "Those damn women. They can dress like women but they behave like men."

I really didn't know very much before at all. I think that I could probably say that I was respectful of diversity and that I wasn't homophobic or transphobic. But I guess it's one thing to intellectualize it and it's another to have to come to terms with a transgender child. Maybe I did have some fear and some of that was just ignorance. One of the things that I just found so helpful was a film that we saw on television about female-to-male transgendered people called, *You Don't Know Dick*. We have met some of Jared's friends and I also work with a woman who has had an incredibly difficult two years because her husband or ex-husband is now transitioning to live life as a woman. I think I try harder to be more understanding and be more open and I think it takes time to truly not be transphobic. I think that I'm getting there or maybe I'm even more there than I just acknowledged. I see transgender people as people first. I also have to say that I have had an extra interest in the world of drag queens and have found it quite fascinating to explore the drag queen culture from the outside looking in.

We do tend to categorize people into either some kind of maleness or some kind of femaleness and I guess that people do want to belong to one or the other gender even though there are so many different variations. I don't know what causes a person to wish to change their gender other than it must be that they don't feel comfortable with who they are externally, and they want to try and make the internal and the external match. I guess my reward is that we will have a child that feels good about himself. It certainly opened my eyes and it's challenged me to truly ask myself how respectful I am of diversity.

I still remember one of my husband's comments when Jared first told us, and now, it kind of makes me laugh. He said, "Why would you want to be a white male in today's society?" It was a great thing to say because Jared spent several years in lesbian activities that were exclusive to women and it just seemed so peculiar to hear him talking about his plans to transition to something that, for a couple of years, in his life he had a hard time relating to—other than selected men who, in a good Yiddish word, were *mensches*.

I wouldn't have been as ready to cope with it if Jared were younger and probably would have been quite fearful about permanent decisions like surgery. I know I would have been absolutely petrified and I was panicked about it enough, even though Jared was older and perhaps more able to think it through. I don't know whether I would feel differently if I had a son who transitioned to female. I certainly know that there are many more men living their lives as women in our city. I'm heartbroken when I hear that some parents can't accept a lesbian daughter or a transgendered child. I actually have that in my own family. I have a first cousin and she and her husband have disowned two daughters because they are lesbians and they've disowned one of their sons because he's supportive of his sisters. I can't imagine that my cousin doesn't see or speak of, or have any knowledge about her children and grandchildren. It's just so tragic that this could happen in my own family. We do need to be asking ourselves why people are so afraid of what they don't understand.

If society was not so phobic, it would be a whole hell of a lot easier. We've gone to Pride Parades with both of our kids for maybe eight or so years. It's a pretty big social event in Vancouver and I heartily clap when the Parent Support Group comes along. But then I also clap pretty heartily when I see the Menopausal Bitches too. So maybe that's just where I'm at in my life as a fifty-six year-old women. I do think that the next generation of young people perhaps will shine in terms of being much more accepting of diversity than my generation. So we'll just have to keep on fighting to hopefully see that light at the end of the tunnel.

Anna was age fifty-five and married. She was born in Canada and had two children. Anna worked as a teacher and in social services and called herself a secular Jewish Humanist. Her daughter, Marla—now Jared—first identified as a lesbian and then disclosed as transgender at age twenty-six in 1996. Anna was involved with progressive and social justice causes including feminism, civil rights, the environment, and peace movements. She was active in local Canadian politics and supportive of LGBT rights. Anna lived in Alaska and was interviewed by mail in 2001.

LOSS

6

Elise

SHE'S A GUY NOW

IT WAS VERY DIFFICULT BECAUSE I loved having a daughter. Loved it. I'm an only child and I didn't have a good relationship with my own mother. She was very distant and so it was just marvelous having a relationship with my daughter and we did a lot together. Even when she went off to graduate school, we always maintained contact. We talked a lot and laughed a lot, and stuff like that.

She, my daughter Justine, was in graduate school when she told me she was in a relationship. I said, "Oh, great!" She said, "But it's with a woman." I asked her if she was a lesbian and she said she just didn't know. So we left it that way. How I found out she thought she was trans was when I decided to get married and wanted her to be my witness. She was beginning to look more masculine. Her hair was getting shorter and she was dressing more masculine-looking and I asked her what would be comfortable to wear to the wedding. That's when she said, "I have to tell you something."

Those words! Whenever your kid says that, you know something is going on. She told me that she thought she was trans and was looking into transition, but she didn't know if she would do it or not. My guess is she knew, but was trying to just go slowly until she was real positive—and not telling me everything right away. When she told me this, I knew she was in a lot of pain because she didn't want me to be in pain. She was very uncomfortable. She cried and, of course, I cried and told her I loved her no matter what. It was a very difficult time for both of us. Her partner just walked out of the room because she didn't want to deal with it. I asked how it would affect their relationship and she said they didn't know. I knew a little bit about transgender issues because of the kind of work I did as a social worker. It wasn't an area of specialization, but I had been to conferences and heard some transgender folks on panels. Actually, they left me feeling very confused.

I asked her a lot of questions and she told me to feel free to ask her anything. I asked what made her think that she was trans. Had she researched it enough? Of course, I knew that she wouldn't do anything in an impulsive way. She said she had been doing some research on the lesbian community when it began. I had brought her up in a very non-sexist way and was very active in the Women's Movement when she was young so she'd always been interested in feminism and women's studies. I'm not sure when she became acquainted with the transgender community or the issue, but I think that through her research and through the books she read, she started to think that maybe this was her. She had met some folks who were transitioning and she identified with them. How they felt.

Then I asked her if she had wished that she were a boy when she was younger because I just never got any indication. I knew she liked sports and didn't like to wear dresses, but I never thought that was odd because I didn't think she needed to wear dresses if she didn't want to. I asked her if it was agonizing. I'd read that it was agonizing for people to feel that they're trapped having to be a certain way. She told me no, and that it was because of me that she didn't have to be boxed in because she was female. One time she did say she wondered what she'd be like if she were a boy. But it wasn't anything that apparently was very troubling.

She just said she felt there was something not quite right. That she always felt that women's clothing just never looked the way they should on her and she wasn't comfortable in them. I said, "Oh my God! It must have been so difficult for you." But she said no and she always did seem to be a happy person. She was never depressed or terribly moody.

It was horrible! It was so painful and I really didn't know how to feel. I didn't know what to do at the beginning because it was a slow thing. She wasn't sure if she was going to have surgery and I felt in limbo for a long time. I didn't really know what to expect and what was going to happen. A lot of my pain too was for my daughter. I wanted her to be happy and I felt this horrible pain about society and the stigma—because transgender people were seen as freakish and weird and strange. I didn't want my daughter to be viewed that way. I didn't want her to be ostracized, prejudiced against.

Remember that movie, *Boys Don't Cry*? It would have been too much for me. I still haven't seen it. I have problems with any kind of violence anyway and it was just too personal for me to see it. I was so worried about violence against my own child. I felt that as a lesbian, she was much more mainstream, and it's not as offensive although people might not be very nice to her if they found her with another female. She did tell me that she and her girlfriend had to be careful because she was in graduate school in the Midwest and it was horrible there. They had all kinds of right wing Christian groups going to the campus and telling them they were sinners and that they were going to die and go to hell. She was also in a class on gay and lesbian issues and brought her class with her to do some counter protesting. I was really worried then. But I felt if she's a lesbian, she's a lesbian. She never thought she would want to have children so it wasn't the dream of grandchildren. I thought if she wanted a child, she could have one.

Transgender seems much more offensive because it's unknown and any time people find someone that's different, they shun them. It's the typical thing that goes on with prejudice, no matter what. If you're different, people are prejudiced against you. I've worked with gay and lesbian youths and I guess, just from being a social worker, I believe in equality for everybody and that you don't dislike people because of their choices. My perspective is probably different from other people because I have two recovering kids. What's really important in life is to have my child sober and alive and well and happy. There were times when both I and her father secretly hoped that this was a phase and that she was a lesbian. I think her father was in denial for a long time after she told him. He had a lot of difficulty with it. But he really loves Justine and said that no matter what, he was always going to love her.

She began taking testosterone. At first, a very small amount of testosterone and then had to increase it because she was getting her period again. So now she's taking larger amounts. I worry about the effect that could have on her body. But there hasn't been any studies so we just don't know. When I asked her about surgery, she told me she was thinking of breast surgery and thought she was going to go through with it. But it was very expensive and she would have to use some of her college loan money. I asked her why it was so important and she said, "Because I can finally get rid of these breasts that I've hated all my life." She was very, very large breasted to the point that when she was a teenager, I had asked her if she wanted to have a breast reduction because it was really horrible and her shoulders were down a lot. But she never liked the thought of surgery back then. Binding herself was very uncomfortable because she was so large and her clothes didn't fit the way she wanted them to. She wanted a trim male look. So it was very important that she have them taken off and that was the point of no return.

When Justine had the surgery, I asked her if she wanted me to go with her, but she thought she'd be more worried about how I was feeling. I was glad because it was better for me not to be there. She had two trans friends who were in different stages go with her. One just had surgery and the other didn't. They brought Justine here after the surgery and she stayed here and I took care of her. When they came here, I made dinner for everybody and we sat around the table and chatted. I got to talk to them and ask questions and just listened to them a lot. I found out that the one who didn't plan on having surgery—she or he or whatever—still does identify herself as a transgendered man. But now that the surgery is done, it's confusing when I remember Justine with her breasts.

Justine really doesn't see herself as a male. But if she had to lean toward something, it would be the male gender. Actually she prefers to be genderless, if there is such a thing. But she goes by the name, Justin and she shops in the men's department to buy clothing. So if she had to lean, it would be towards being a male. I feel kind of in limbo because of the pronouns and what to use and she, herself, is not sure. I do believe that sexuality is on a spectrum. Not everybody is all this or all that, and the same thing with gender. Maybe in twenty-five, thirty, or fifty years, our society won't need to use those types of pronouns.

I'm very open about it because that's just my philosophy. I don't like to live a lie. I did check with her about needing to talk with my friends and that was okay with her. I also told two elderly aunts, but they didn't show any kind of reaction. They're in their early eighties and I don't think they quite understood. She seems to be staying away from them and from family gatherings on her father's side. I don't think that he has said anything to any of them. I did tell my priest before the wedding, just to not have embarrassment on his part, because my daughter would be one of my witnesses and that she was going to look pretty masculine. Which she did. She was dressed very masculine. My priest was wonderful. I belong to a very liberal, progressive parish. It's the only way I would stay there. They're very open and affirming to people who are gay and lesbian and transgender and it's brought up a lot in prayers to help stop prejudice.

But I will say I'm still having some after-effects of grief. It's hard for me to talk about this again. I guess I've been having a slump. I'm not quite sure why. Maybe I'm not accepting that it's okay to be in a slump. I was doing quite well and then her birthday came around and I had to buy a birthday card. Her birthday was hard. I spent a lot of time looking for an appropriate card. A daughter card didn't feel appropriate. A son card didn't feel appropriate. I didn't want to just give her any kind of a birthday card because she is my daughter. So I found something about that she was the high spot in our family and she thought it was kind of funny that she would be the high spot. She said a lot of people wouldn't think that.

I did go to PFLAG at first, maybe six or seven times. No more because I was so busy and I felt that overall, I was doing okay. I did go back for a while because I met another mother of a daughter who was trans. But she and I were the only ones and when we would break out in small groups, it was just too different and I didn't feel they could understand. It was like, "Oh, my goodness! Wow!" That sort of thing. Our issues were just different. But I would love to be in some kind of a support group.

When I said the issues were different, I meant losing a child of a particular gender. If my daughter were a lesbian, it would be okay. I mean what do you do with those pictures of the child dressed as a girl? Easter was really hard because I used to make her dresses and now, what do I do with those pictures with all those little dresses? That's a loss. How do I relate to this child now that she identifies as a different gender? I certainly relate to my son differently than my daughter although I brought him up in a very non-sexist way. When my daughter and I would go traveling together, we would stay in the same room. It wasn't a big deal. I wouldn't be comfortable doing that now. She's a guy now. I wouldn't do that with my son. We never walked around naked all the time, but I would go in the bathroom while she was taking a shower. There are just boundaries with sons that start at a certain age and are different for daughters.

We never did girlie things together. She never was that interested in perfumes and powders and the lotions and makeup. Not that I do a lot of that either. But we used to go to the mall and have a ball with all these coupons. It was very difficult shopping with her at first when she began to go to the men's department. That was hard for me. Then when she started going into men's dressing rooms, it was just, "My goodness!" Before I'd be calling, "Justine, are you in there?" I would be looking in the dressing rooms. Now what do I do? I can't go in there. Call out Justin? So many things you never think of.

I just don't really know what the new rules are. We always used to joke about bio men. But I'm looking at somebody that looks like a guy and it's just not the same thing. Of course, I mean you can joke about bio men with gay men, which I've done. But it's not the same with her. When we were both dating guys and were having trouble with our relationships at the same time, we would just laugh about them and have so much fun about how bio men act. I do know that the affection is a little different. I give her a big hug and a kiss, but she'll do the hug and cheek kind of thing. She says it's not different, but I think it is. She's not as affectionate and that's okay, I guess. Another loss. She just seems to be different. Her voice is lower too because of testosterone. Maybe it's the testosterone or maybe it's because of her identifying as a different gender. I'm not sure.

This is my child, yes. But my child's an adult and again, I still don't know how to refer to her because I'm not really comfortable saying my child. I don't know what to say anymore. I always wanted to be close. I didn't get that kind of nurturing and emotional availability that would have been nice to have. My mom was a real intrusive type mom and I didn't want to be intrusive and try to impose on my kids what I thought they should do with their lives. That they had to go to this college, or they would have to do that with their lives, or they would have to have children. I've been the kind of mother that's pretty accepting. I decided that was how I wanted to be. Accept them, give them their space, give them the confidence that whatever they'd do, they'd make the right decisions and I'd support them. That's what happened when Justin told me that she was going to transition. I think that's the thing I'm proudest of.

I wasn't going to make the mistake of telling them how they should live their lives. I can give my opinion, if they ask me. I can tell my son that I think he's not making the best choices in his life because of drinking. But then I have to pull back and go on with my life. I have a lot of pain over my son's drinking problem. I worry more about him than I do about Justine at this point in time. Because she, I hope, will be okay. She is very aware of making sure she's in safe situations. She's not one that would be going in bars or flaunting anything. She's an activist, but she's not going to be an in-your-face kind of person.

I wish I could have been more available for them and had more emotional energy when they were growing up. But my mother had a lot of problems so I was dealing with her and then I went back to school. So I think if I hadn't gone back to school and not become a feminist and if I had been Susie Homemaker, my marriage would have been fine. But I know that's not so. I wasn't a cookies and milk kind of mother, but I did go to their games. I would bring my books with me and when they were up at bat, I would put them down and watch and clap. Then I could go back to my books. But I made her dresses for Easter and baked and cooked and tried to juggle it all and deal with an emotionally disturbed mother. Trying to be Superwoman, I guess. It zapped a lot of my energy and I may not have been as open and accepting when they were little. That's my regret. If I had to do it over again, it would have been nice to have been able to finish school before I got married and then I would have been more available. I'm hard on myself. I always expect more of myself.

I did wonder, because I gave birth to a child that is now transgendered, if there was something I might have done when she was in utero. Like if one experiences anything traumatic, or is under a lot of stress so that something is messed up in some way. When I was pregnant with Justine, it was a very stressful time with my own mother and her alcoholism and emotional problems. There were times she'd say horrible things to me like she was going to come over and put a knife in my stomach. I was just so traumatized and just couldn't say, "Fuck you! I'm never talking to you again!" And hang up. I needed to be this understanding person so I just cried and cried and was so upset. Of course, the next day she'd be sober and tell me she never said that. Did that woman's alcoholism affect my child? It was bad enough that it affected me. Was there something that could have happened with hormones or chemicals that could have messed something up in utero?

It's just not enough to have the pressure of being a wonderful mother when they're born. You have to be concerned even during pregnancy and I'm not talking about diet. I think about how many women were pregnant during war and gave birth under awful, awful circumstances. But they produced proportionately greater heterosexual children. Not homosexual or transgender children. So who knows? I really don't want to look at cause, but there's this whole phase that adds androgynization in utero and maybe there's a range. Every embryo is structurally a female and then androgen comes in to masculinize—or much less to feminize. Maybe there's turning points where somebody who is genetically female is more or less androgynized and there's just degrees along the way.

I can't have my whole life hinge on the decisions my kids are making. It's kind of like detachment, but not less loving. I can still love them and accept them. Maybe I'm accepting to a fault. Maybe I'm denying my own feelings and delaying my own process by putting aside how I feel. I always feel I should just adjust and adapt. We haven't had as much contact lately as we had before. But we still touch base at least once a week. I think we were very dependent on each other. Maybe she especially, but now she's moving on. Maybe she needs distance or she's just very busy in her own life and needs to connect with me less. I think I need some distance too. There's still a connection, but right now I feel like I don't need to spend a lot of time with her. So that's a loss too.

At the beginning, I was very thirsty for any information I could get and would go online and try to connect with other people although I wasn't really that successful. I may try again. But then I feel I've had enough. I have to put this away for a while. I do have another life. This doesn't have to be all consuming. My kids have their own lives. They make their decisions and I can only accept the decisions they make and love them. That's all I can do. I can't do anything else.

Elise, age fifty-six, was divorced and remarried. She was a social worker and identified herself as Catholic. She had two children. Her child Justine—now Justin—came out as a lesbian at twenty-three and then as transgender at age thirty in 1998. Elise said she was a feminist and had been active in the civil rights and anti-war movements. She had attended PFLAG meetings, but found the discussions not especially relevant to her as a mother of a transgender child. Elise lived in Connecticut and was interviewed in 2001.

7

Mariam

ALL THOSE WEDDINGS, ALL THOSE SHOWERS

I THINK I KNEW BEFORE SHE TOLD ME. But I kept hoping it wasn't so. The make-up came off. She began wearing these way-out clothes. She cropped her hair and she actually moved in with a lesbian couple. Then she started making fun of our family. The wedding receptions. The showers. The get-togethers. I'd have to beg her to go. With both our families, my husband's and mine, it's an obligation. There's no question that you don't go. My husband was very worried. He talked about the kind of magazines she was bringing home. That she wasn't living in a good environment. But he didn't say anything else. I did bring it up to her one time. She said not to worry. That I'd be the first to know.

Leila, my daughter—now she wants to be called Lee—was always kind of a tomboy right from the beginning. No interest in dolls or nice clothes. But I thought she'd get over it once she was a teenager and became interested in boys. So I was suspicious. But even though I suspected, I was so shocked. I was devastated. Just blown out of the water. It was so foreign. So weird. I guess I kind of cracked up. I couldn't feel worse if she died. It was horrible to feel that way. All my hopes and expectations—gone. But there was one good thing. I understood why she had become so detached.

I called my sister. Then her father. I must have called my daughter a million times, asking her all kind of questions. Why? Why? Because she was brought up in a father-dominated home? My husband's pretty macho. A kind of take charge guy. Because he put me down? Because I let him? Because she didn't want to be like me? Because she wanted to be like him? Identify with him. That's the kind of thoughts I was thinking. We wanted her to see a psychiatrist. She wanted us to see a psychiatrist.

She would come home and the way she dressed! Jeans and boots. Her short hair. I didn't know what to tell my family. I was so embarrassed. I was so ashamed. I know them. What they'll think of us as parents. Say about us. Talking about us when we're not there. Gossiping. Feeling sorry for us. At first, her father ignored it. Then he told her if she couldn't dress properly and be circumspect, to not bother to come home. It broke my heart. Of course, she comes home, but not so often and she and my husband are so stiff and tense together. Not saying much of anything. Not even small talk. We live in a big house, but not that big. I know it broke his heart too. After all, she was his little girl.

My husband and I both come from very traditional families. Both our families are Lebanese. Christian Orthodox. Very religious. Very conventional. Critical of American ways. You know, modern ways, especially when it comes to raising children. We believe in strictness, that children need to conform, be obedient. Americans give their children too much freedom. We raise our children to stay Lebanese. To stay close to family. To be part of the Lebanese community. It's very hard with my family. I come from a very big family. My family is very close. Almost all of my social life is my family. That's the way we are. My father has passed away, but I'm very close to my mother. With everyone. Aunts, uncles, cousins, Godparents. There's no way they'd understand or accept. Can you understand this? They cannot know. We'd be a pariah. We'd lose all respect in the Lebanese community. We'd lose our standing if it ever got out. Not just us. Our family. My family. My husband's family. Everyone. I would die from shame.

My mother has no idea. She still calls my daughter a tomboy. My husband blames me. Says I was too lenient letting her do whatever she wanted. Maybe I did. Maybe I wanted to raise her different. Not so strict, not so many rules like I was raised with. My in-laws? They would blame me because I let her go to school away from home. That I let her live on her own after she graduated college. That I made her be a bad role model for her girl cousins. I let her do this? Where was my husband? I'll never hear the end of it. My family believes that children, especially girls, should live at home until they're married. Of course to a nice Lebanese husband. They keep asking me about a boyfriend and I say, "Not yet." The one sister I told, she keeps saying that Leila will change back. That she's so beautiful, she can get any guy she wants. That she'll meet a guy. But I don't think so.

I'm afraid for her. I think that she'll be lonely. Discriminated against. On the fringe. I'm afraid she'll be attacked. I'm afraid of people pointing fingers at her. I can't stand being around her friends. When I go to see her, I don't know what to do with myself. She lives with all these women. They all look like guys. I don't know what to say to them. They all look so masculine. Constantly putting down men, but they seem to want to look like men. Don't they like being women? There is this one girl who I think is her girlfriend. She brought her home just once. But she hasn't told me. I don't get it. But she's happy. I know she's happy. I just don't get it. I don't understand her life. I don't know what she does. Where she goes.

It has affected my relationship with my husband. When I told him, he didn't say much. He just told me he didn't want to talk about it anymore. And that's where it stands. He won't talk about it. So what does it do to a marriage when you can't talk about something so important? When I can't tell him what's bothering me. He was never big on feelings. So I'm all alone with this. I'm so angry with him. His head is in the sand. Goes to work. Works all the time and comes home and goes to sleep. My son knows something is wrong, but he doesn't ask. I know it's taking a big toll on my marriage. I don't want to sleep with my husband anymore. I mean have sex with him. Maybe it's my anger. But when he tries, I think of my daughter. I think of women having sex together. I can't help it. One good thing about going to PFLAG was that a couple of times some of the women talked about this. Losing interest in sex. You know, I'm not the only one. Before I heard other mothers talk about it, I thought I was just going crazy.

I can't seem to make peace with it. All those weddings. All those showers. Me being a grandmother. I feel ripped off. I feel rejected. She's like a stranger. We used to be so close. Especially when she was a little kid. I took her everywhere with me. I loved having a little girl and I thought we'd always have such a close and special relationship. I thought she would marry and have children and that I'd be a grandmother. I thought we'd talk about jewelry and clothes and go on vacations together and she'd be a part of our family, like her cousins. Now we're so far apart. We don't know what to talk about anymore. She doesn't want to be alone with me. What it comes down to is this. She's not comfortable in traditional situations. I'm not comfortable in lesbian situations. What do we do? Where do we go?

I go to PFLAG, but it really doesn't help. The people there seem to just want you to accept and get on with it. They can't really understand my situation with my family. Or what my husband is like. They don't know what it's like to be Lebanese. I go to therapy. I go to a mother's group. It's better than PFLAG because it's just a few of us and we really do talk. But it doesn't change anything. She's still a lesbian. My family is my family. My husband isn't going to change. My daughter and I aren't going to be any closer. What can change? We're in different worlds. That's the way I feel. How can I feel any different? Maybe one day, you just wake up and it's all right. But I don't think so. Look at what she's left me with. Pretense with my family. Unhappiness in my marriage. No more real daughter and a life of worry and secrets. That's what she's left me with.

Mariam, age fifty-six, had worked briefly as a secretary prior to her marriage. She had two children. Her daughter Leila disclosed that she was a lesbian at age twenty-two in 1988. Although Mariam had attended PFLAG *meetings, she felt she was being pushed to accept her daughter's lesbianism and that the other parents could not understand the traditional values and obligations of her Lebanese-American family—and the social consequences of Leila's sexual orientation. Mariam lived in Massachusetts and was interviewed in 1990.*

8

Jenny

HE'S GONNA LOSE EVERYTHING EXCEPT HIS PARENTS

I LOVED THIS CHILD, BUT I WAS ALSO VERY ANGRY because she was always so depressed. Growing up, she didn't have any friends and that was hard. She would come home from school and go up to her room. Buried herself in books and always working on homework. I told her that if there was somebody in her class that was also kind of ostracized and who also needed a friend, to invite her over for lunch or something. I encouraged her to befriend other people that were having trouble finding friends too. I thought if she couldn't be with the popular group, she could be with another group and have some friends. But now Andrew has lots of friends. Lots. Lots of boyfriends. He went through several boyfriends before he found his partner.

I had tried to help her feel better about herself. We went together to get our ears pierced. I was always painting her fingernails, trying to get her interested in playing with dolls, dressing up in my clothes. Actually, I found out that my son also liked nail polish and wanted to dress up in my clothes. I mean my son did all the same female things that my daughter was doing. But it never made my son feminine in any way and it never made my daughter feminine either. When she was little, I kept her hair long. She had such pretty hair and I always put ruffled pretty things on her. "Hey," I thought. "This is my little girl. This is my ruffled, flowery little girl that I've always wanted." When she first went to school, I got her this very expensive beautiful red jacket with flowers all over. She absolutely refused to wear it. She said, "I don't like flowers."

Then my parents and my parent's friends were all saying how wonderful it was to have grandchildren. I was looking forward to someday being a grandparent too. Then at the age of about fourteen when Andrew was just starting her period and beginning to develop, we had some very serious talks because she was saying she didn't want to wear a bra and that she hated the fact that she was developing. I kept thinking back to when I and my friends were in the sixth grade and stuffing our bras with tissues. And here was this child that needed to wear a bra and I had to fight to get her to wear one. When she started having her period, she hated it. I had talks with her, saying, "If you're getting your period, you'll be able to be a mom, to get pregnant, to have a baby." She said, "I never want a baby inside me. It sounds awful. If I ever have kids, I would adopt, but I don't really know if I want kids." I mean this is at fifteen years old. She had a very hard time with her period. Terrible cramps and really fought going to a doctor to check it out. She didn't like doctors and she didn't like shots. Now she's giving herself shots all the time.

I really had no idea. But after she told me she was going to be male, I looked back and could remember all the signs. I mean he was always different. There was nothing female about him. He wanted his hair all chopped off. Always wearing raggedy boy's clothes. Never having any girlfriends. As a child, when he was female, sometimes he was taken for a male. He was so happy about it and hated it if I corrected them. I just put it all in the wrong box. I thought it was because she was jealous of her brother. That she thought her brother had it better. Maybe she thought I liked her brother better, or I liked boys better than girls. I don't think I treated her any less than I treated her brother. I kept reassuring her that I really wanted a daughter. Maybe she wanted to be a man instead of a woman because men have better jobs. Men get paid more.

She told us, my husband and I, at the same time. I started crying right away, saying, "What do you mean? What are you talking about?" My husband tried to comfort me. He said to her, "You're our child. We'll always love you." I said, "That's true, but you're my daughter. I always thought you were going to be my daughter. I love you, but how can you feel this way? I've never heard of this before." Both my husband and I knew about Christine Jorgensen and Rene Richards. But we never heard of going from female to male. But he said that he had gone to therapy and the therapist got it out of him how he felt and then told him that it was possible. But I was still back at "It's not possible. You can't be a male!"

When she told us, she said she was always a gay male. She said at about the age of eight or nine, she realized that she liked guys, but she also felt like a guy. She didn't really have the words to describe it. She did go for counseling back then, but she never told any therapist her feelings because she said, if she did, they would have thought she was crazy and sent her to a mental institution. That was one of the biggest fears that he had. But I was thinking that this is a stage. This is going to pass. Next time we see him, he's going to tell us that it's not going to happen.

I started looking up literature right away, trying to find something out about it. One of the first books I read was about Rene Richards, but there was hardly anything to read about women wanting to change to be male. The first article that I found was in *The New Yorker* called, "The Body Lies" that actually talked about females to males. Then my son showed me how to search on the Internet. There was very little on the Internet then, but it was shortly thereafter that I found other mothers and other transgender people. It was devastating because the stories were so tear-jerking. They told about how hard their lives were and how hard it was to transition. I just thought this is such a terrible thing. I didn't know why this child who had so much and so much going for her, loved by parents and family, could be like this. Could want to change their gender. My child can't do this, I thought. He's gonna lose everything except his parents. I'd lose my friends. My parents and in-laws would have nothing more to do with him. I mean you have to be out with your family. I had so many worries and concerns, but as each situation passed, it worked out so much better than I ever thought.

I still called him as often as usual. But I was noticing that his voice was kind of deep and scratchy. I said, "What's the matter with your voice? What's going on?" He said he had a cold and the cold lingered and lingered until he finally came home, maybe six weeks later, and his voice was much deeper. He told us he'd seen a therapist and that he was starting on hormones. I said, "How could you start on hormones? How could you do this to your body? You don't know what you're doing." He said that he had talked with his therapist for a long time and that he knew exactly what he was doing. His therapist said that he needed to change. I said to him, "What gives this person the right to tell you that? This person can't make you change. You don't have to change. We love you the way you are." Then he got the big shoulders. He asked us to check out his shoulders.

Actually he came to me then and said, "I've chosen Andrew as my name because it's closest to the name you gave me." But I didn't really care at the time. Maybe if he had told me later. But his new name, Andrew, was fine with me. My whole family was just wonderful. I had a problem with one brother-in-law who said to Andrew, "How could you do this to your dad?" My husband overheard and said, "It doesn't bother us. You shouldn't let it bother you." And my brother-in-law said, "Oh, okay. Then it doesn't bother me." That was the closest we had to anyone in the family rejecting him. But I worried. My child won't be able to find a job. He'll never have a partner. He was married back then so he also was getting a divorce. I thought that he's never going to have anybody that will love him. Anybody that he can love. He's always gonna be by himself.

Andrew wanted me to meet his therapist so I went with him with chips on both shoulders. I went in there and said, "Who do you think you are? What are you doing to my child?" I was really, really angry, but this therapist talked with me for a long time and told me about a support group. I went to the support group and I saw about fifteen other people that were just like Andrew. I listened to their stories and it brought back what I had read. These people were just like the people in the books. They had to do this.

So I sort of came away with a little more understanding. But I was thinking, where are all these people's parents? Couldn't these parents help their kids so they wouldn't have to do this? Am I the only parent that is letting my child do this? I've got to meet other parents. I want to talk to other parents and I asked Andrew if he knew of any other parents. Did any of his friends have parents that would talk to me? The group that Andrew was going to, they were all in their forties and fifties. But there was one sixteen year old. She looked like a high school cheerleader and at first, I didn't realize that she was a male to female. I mean this was a cheerleading type gal. She was darling. I wanted to meet this person's parents. But they wouldn't meet with me. They wouldn't talk to me.

Andrew was living away from home, but he came back and lived with us for a while. He was pretty lonely. He said, "Mom, I have to move back because that's where I find support and people like me." I said, "Well, you don't have to go. Let's start a support group here. You'll meet new people here. Don't go back." So we started a support group. Andrew knew somebody that knew somebody. I, somehow, met the mother of a male to female child who was in her fifties. The mother was like in her seventies. She was really a neat lady and very supportive. We talked and I said, "I would like to get a group together of parents. Would you like to help me and come to this group?" And she did. There were six of us at the first meeting. The next time there must have been maybe ten. The next meeting was twenty people and the next meeting was thirty people and it just grew. It's been pretty steady between fifty and sixty people every month.

I loved my child. I wanted to make things better for him. I'm a people person. I'm very social. I wanted to educate people. Every little group I go to, I tell more people. Then that's more people that might understand and might help someone else understand. I always feel so good when I help some mother who was so upset to start to feel better. I used to go out and speak. But I would still get teary as I was talking about it and it took quite a while until I stopped being teary-eyed. The one thing that still emotionally hurts me is why he never said anything sooner. So I could have made his life better than it was. I don't know that it would have been any easier for me, but at least I wouldn't have forced all these female things on him. Well, I understand that they are worried about telling somebody really close because they don't want to lose that person. They don't want that person to reject them and I'm sure my child was worried about us rejecting him. Or couldn't tell me how and why she rejected all this female stuff that I wanted for her.

But I do wish I would have known about Andrew sooner. I

think it would have been easier for all of us. I mean, she could sometimes be so mean and nasty especially to her brother that I don't think they'll ever be close. It's better now than when she was female, but it's still not great. They both live in the same city, but they don't see each other except when we come down to do stuff together with them. My husband had a very poor relationship with Andrew. She was not the little girl he thought he was going to have. He even said to me a couple of times that I was going to have to be her best friend because he couldn't deal with her. But after Andrew transitioned, he was just a better person and he and my husband could talk a little better. They even did a couple of male type bonding things, just the two of them, which my husband would have never done when she was his daughter.

Andrew's never been harassed. One time my husband and I were taking him out to dinner and while we were in the restaurant, he said, "I have to go to the bathroom. Should I use the girls' bathroom?" My husband said, "Don't you use the men's bathroom?" And he said, "No, I never have. I've been too afraid." And my husband said, "Well, I'll make sure nobody's in there so you can go in." And that's what they did. My husband went in to make sure nobody was in there and then Andrew went in. Later Andrew said, "I can't believe he came in and was using the urinal while I was in there."

There's been a lot of changes. Like one time Andrew was in the bedroom talking with me and I started getting undressed. He said, "Mom, I'm not the same daughter you used to have. You probably shouldn't undress in front of me." I said, "Well, you're still my kid. Don't look if you don't want to see." Now he doesn't like clothes. One time I asked him to come shopping with me. That I needed him to help me pick something out and he said, "I don't like to go in the women's department. You know that." I said, "Well, you're not buying something for yourself. You're helping me." He said, "I don't want to do that."

I think I was a good mother because I loved my kids so. I always fought for them. Anytime they had some kind of problem at school, I would go and say, "You can't do this to my child." I think that we provided them with all kinds of wonderful opportunities and we did a lot of traveling. Lots of family vacations. Even when my husband was working hard, I told him that he had to come home one night a week. I encouraged us to be a close family. Whenever our kids had a party or an activity at school, we were both always there. I did wonder if it was something I did when I was pregnant. Did I take a medication that caused his brain to be male and his body to be female? I still wonder, but I know it's nothing I can be concerned about. I didn't do anything intentionally.

I know someone whose son murdered his wife and this mother accepted her child and still loved him more than any of the mothers of children who have transitioned. These people sold their home and everything to put up the money for bail and the best attorneys. Parents of kids who are good and wonderful people, they wouldn't give them a cent towards hormones or therapy or surgery. Yet, a kid who's a bad person, a druggie or murderer or commits any kind of crime, the parents will do anything to pay for an attorney and what not. One thing I will say is that I'll never understand it. I'll never understand him or the process or anything. But you don't have to understand it to accept it. I know how I feel about myself and my body and I wouldn't want to change my body. I can't understand somebody wanting to do that. I can't understand people that lose their families and children and parents and do it anyway. I mean there must be something so oppressing that they have to do this. I feel that it's either a choice between suicide or transitioning. Mostly I regret not having more children. That's a big regret. Not having more children. Because maybe then I could still have a daughter.

Jenny, age fifty-seven, was married, had worked as a teacher, and said that her religious affiliation was Reform Judaism. Jenny had two children. Her child Andrea—now Andrew—had been married and disclosed as transgender at age twenty-three in 1991. He was in a long term relationship with another man and identified as a gay male. Jenny had established one of the first on-line informational and support groups for parents of trans and trans people and was a nationally known activist and leader in the transgender civil right movement. She lived in Ohio and was interviewed in 2001.

9
Lisa

I MISS THE PERSON HE WAS WHEN HE WAS A SHE

IT SHOULDN'T HAVE SURPRISED ME BECAUSE Nathan had always been a very aggressive and competitive person. She played basketball and ran track and played volleyball and rugby and always excelled at everything. I didn't realize it back then, but there were a lot of signs that she was more male than female. When her eighth grade prom came around, one of my friends gave her a beautiful dress, even though she never liked to be dressed in dressy kind of things, and she got all mad because we made her wear makeup. We almost had to sit on her to take a picture and it was one of my favorites. She was just beautiful and it was kind of hard to see her become a guy, although she is a very handsome young man.

She had come out as a lesbian the summer before her senior year of high school. She was very dyke-ish and cut her hair very short and had a very androgynous way of dressing and it was difficult to tell whether she was a male or female because she always wore a sports bra which didn't accentuate her breasts. She had pretty much secluded herself before she came out and although I didn't know it at the time, one of her friends had outed her and she went through some pretty difficult times at school. That changed her outlook and her opinions of people and that was sad. I went through all of the typical parental torments. It's my fault. What have I done wrong? But she seemed to do much better when she went away to college.

I've always considered myself to be an open-minded person. When she came out as a lesbian, one thing I had to remind myself of was that I had always taught my children that no matter what someone's orientation, color, religion or beliefs, they're to be respected. It's that person's right. What helped was that we were so very fond of her partner who is still a part of our family even though they broke up several years ago. So that made it easier because she brought a wonderful person into our lives. But it was harder when she came out as trans. I had to really take a dose of my own medicine.

The first indication of Nathan's intention to transition was about three years ago when she told me she was changing her name. At first, I was very against it because of all the children I named, hers was my favorite name. From that point on, I knew that she was looking towards being identified as a more male-gendered female. But the new middle name she chose was the last name of one of my very best friends who is a lesbian. In fact, she and her partner call themselves Nathan's fairy dyke mothers. So Nathan honored them by choosing that name.

When she told me, she asked if I knew what transgendered was. I'm not naïve. I watch television and knew about people who felt that they were born in the wrong body. I told her that I knew what it was and she said that she always felt that she was not right and wanted to change and start taking hormones. My first concern was medical. Was it safe? Was this something that was going to harm her physically? Was she going to change her mind? Was this a phase? You have to understand that, to Nathan, shocking people was always one of her favorite things. So I was a little apprehensive about her decision and I was so disappointed. When I say disappointed, it has to do with being a female, being a woman. It was sad simply because here was this aggressive, smart, and beautiful woman that could have done good things for womankind and made a difference in the world.

I didn't see her again for another year and when we talked on the telephone, I noticed that her voice was sounding more and more male. Hoarse, like she had a cold. So that took some getting used to. Then she began to tell me about lifting weights and doing pull-ups and she also became vegan which I think disturbed me more than anything. I don't know why. We had visited some friends of hers and they were all using a male pronoun in reference to her, or to him, and I wasn't quite ready for that. When I think of everything that I've had to get used to, the most difficult part of the transition was using male pronouns and calling Nathan him and his and he. I still have to catch myself and to be honest, I don't like to refer to him that way. So I generally opt to say Nathan and not he. That's easier for me. Anyways, this is all still pretty new to us.

When Nathan finished college, we all went to his graduation. It was supposed to be a celebration, but his life was pretty much in turmoil. She had broken up with her girlfriend and had some new roommates so it was not comfortable for all of us to be there and we got a motel room. It was apparent that time together was not going to be that enjoyable and I don't think he necessarily wanted us to be there. He was going through some pretty trying times as well as graduating and getting ready for his new life.

He was very determined that we accept him as a male and respect his decision. When we got there, her appearance had not changed too much other than she was beginning to have broader shoulders and you could see the effects of the hormones. But the part that was the most difficult was that Nathan seemed unwilling to give people time. We were immediately to say him, he, his, and call him Nathan. If one of his sisters slipped and called her, called him Natalie or Nat, he wouldn't answer. He would become pretty belligerent and I felt like that was kind of unfair. I would like transgender individuals to understand how their parents are feeling, to give them time to come around, a little room to get used to the idea, and to not think that we don't understand or love them. As one of my daughters put it, "You've been my sister for twenty years and I've always loved you as my sister and it's hard for me to think of you now as my brother." And Nathan was just unwilling to allow for that space.

I know that it was difficult and very harrowing for him to make this decision and to come to terms with that he was a man in a woman's body and that it needed to be changed for her to be happy and fulfilled. I think I'd probably be okay with it if she seemed happy and fulfilled. However, I just don't think that he is because there was one change in Nathan that had nothing to do with her orientation or her transgender appearance. The biggest thing was the pessimism. Her demeanor. Her attitude. She had always been a very fun and happy person. The kind of person you loved to be around. A very charged individual. When you were around her, you could feel the life in her. But she had become dark and quiet and the music that she chose to listen to was very pessimistic. You know, the world is out to get you and so be on guard. To me, it was a bizarre attitude and the veganism made it twice as bad. I had never experienced that before with her and was truly upset.

But even though he had this negative attitude, he was getting his Master's Degree and doing really well in school. He did have some problems when he began graduate school. I think that the faculty was surprised because there were recommendations from her undergraduate professors when she was a she and they probably were a little put off by the transgender change. At any rate, he still has this darker attitude and feeling about life. He's still more withdrawn than ever and not as happy and that bothers me a lot. Not only do I miss my daughter, but I miss that individual. I miss the person he was when he was a she. It would be okay with me if he was a he and he was back to being that happy-go-lucky kind of person he was. When she was Natalie, she was the most entertaining thing we had and everyone loved her. I hope that's not going to change.

When we next saw him, he really appeared male. We went to visit my fiancé's family, and his sister-in-law who had known Nathan quite well, whispered, "Who's that guy?" She really was passing and there was no question that Nathan now looked like a young man. It was sad because we've always been a pretty close-knit family so it was painful to feel like I had lost her. We do still have a good relationship and talk on the phone once a week. Whenever she's feeling down or feeling put upon and the world's just crashing in, he'll give me a call and we'll talk. But even though it's been well over a year, I still find it very difficult to accept my daughter as a male. However, I'm working on it because it is his decision. It is what he wants. Bottom line is if this makes Nathan happy, then this is how it should be. I just hope that it does.

I raised my children in a very dysfunctional home. I married very young and the kids' dad was an addict so I pretty much raised them by myself. I was determined to depart from my family history which was that girls graduated high school, if they were lucky, and got married, had children, and went to work at Woolworth's or Walmart. I wanted better things for my daughters and I was very determined to make them aware that it was important to be independent and to stand on their own two feet before getting married and settling down. I always said that they were not done with school when they graduated high school and all of them went on to college.

In terms of my family, it has been a very difficult adjustment. Nathan spent some time with my mother and she was doing his laundry and saw some men's underwear and my sister told her she thought Nathan was a lesbian. At any rate, we're about to come to a very difficult time. My older daughter and I are both getting married and all our families are going to the wedding and then on a five-day cruise and, of course, Nathan is included. He now shaves and his facial hair has begun to come in so he has a goatee and I feel certain that he is fully passing as a male. My parents who are a little old fashioned are going to find this very alarming and I'm going down to see them and prepare them because it's better that we let them try to get used to this and accept Nathan as male rather than shocking them later. My biggest fear is that my family is going to have a hard time accepting Nathan as he is now and I'm concerned with how they're going to react and how that's going to affect him. I don't want him hurt. I don't want him to feel that he's not okay and not a part of the family. But I do remember how difficult it was for me at first and I love him unconditionally. So I can imagine how difficult it's going to be for them.

One thing about Nathan is that she tends to have a real need to educate people about what he is and how this change came about. He asked me if he should help explain things to my parents and I told him that he really shouldn't be there because it was going to be shocking enough for them just to hear about it, never mind see it. But Nathan has a tendency to want to expound on everything. It's like when she came out to me as a lesbian and said that if I had any questions about what lesbians do, I should just let him know. How I answered was, "I don't ever want to know what you do in the privacy of your room, lesbian or heterosexual or whatever. That's personal and private and I don't need to know that." As a straight person, I don't want to know what other straight couples do. To me it's a very private thing. Still as a transgender, she has a tendency to really want us to know all of the intimate details.

She would like to have the upper part of her body changed to male, but she can't afford it and her insurance won't cover it. Although that's difficult for me to accept, if she's going to transition to become a male, I really would prefer that she take these steps to feel normal, whatever normal is in terms of that. I do know that he is planning to do it as soon as he can afford it. In terms of real world fears, Nathan is just horrified about lying and people finding out. I think a lot of that has to do with a movie about Teena Brandon or Brandon Teena who was transgendered and murdered. I watched the movie because Nathan was just so adamant that we could not slip up and call him her in public, because if people knew, they might try to hurt him. But in terms of that movie, I don't think it was the fact that he was a she, but rather that she stole someone's girlfriend. A transgendered person should not have to say, "Hi, I'm Nathan. I'm transgendered." They should be able to be themselves and it's really no one else's business.

There are times when Nathan travels alone and I do worry and wonder if someone would be rude enough or horrible enough to hurt him and I'm frightened because of the way that he responds to people. Transgender individuals need to understand that the decision that they have made is not one that mainstream America, and well most other countries, generally accept unconditionally. But I think that he's going to be okay as long as he remembers to be basically honest with people, even though I know that's hard to do when your biological sex is female and you're presenting yourself as a male.

Nathan's biological father still has no idea. I think he knows that she's a lesbian, but they really don't have much contact. His relationship with him, well, there is none. I think he's in jail right now and doesn't contact any of the children. A letter every now and then, but that's about it. In terms of my fiancé, Dan, there was a problem at first because my whole life revolved around my children. When that changed and Dan and I began to have a relationship, Nathan was pretty jealous and they had a competition sort of thing going that was pretty uncomfortable. Nathan was always very possessive of me and didn't like sharing me at all.

But Dan has been her dad for ten years and he's been every bit of a father to Nathan. More so than her own father ever was. He's been really wonderful with all of them. I did not tell him about Nathan transitioning when I first heard, simply because I really felt he was not going to accept it. When she first came out as a lesbian, Dan thought it was strange, but it didn't seem to bother him too much and it didn't affect our relationship. In terms of the transitioning, I can only say what I think he's feeling. I think he's hurt by losing a daughter and that he may have been feeling a lot of the same things that I have. But he doesn't really understand. He still loves Nathan and if she calls and tells him she needs something, he's the first person to give it to her, be it money—which it generally is. However, he is very adamant about using the female pronoun although he will call her Nathan.

The problem I'm having is that I believe we need to love all of our children, no matter what their decisions as long as they're not hurting themselves or someone else. Be it color their hair pink or be transgendered or whatever. Dan's having a hard time and sometimes I just have to tell him to be quiet because of his negative responses, so that is affecting us. It's something we can't talk about. In the past we've always been able to talk about anything and everything, but this is something that we don't see eye to eye on, so we avoid it and that's not good. I think that my children are reasonably well accepting of others, although not always of their own siblings. My other son who is fifteen has been pretty nonchalant and seems to not be too concerned. My older daughter is bewildered, but tries very hard to respect Nathan and to use his name and the right pronouns. But she has a hard time being open with her friends in terms of people who knew Nathan when Nathan was Natalie. My other daughter is absolutely belligerent and adamant and of all of the family, tends to be the hardest on Nathan and the least willing to accept it. I think a lot of that is personal between the two of them so that's kind of expected. On the cruise, everybody is kind of doubling up in rooms and she's already said that it would make her uncomfortable to room with

Nathan. So we really haven't felt the full effect of how Nathan's transition will be on all of us.

She has a very close knit group which I'm very glad of. A very supportive family and in terms of family, I mean gay and transgendered individuals who support him and they spend a lot of time doing things together. I think that's really important and he still has sports. However, I think he limits himself to running because he no longer can participate in sports with female teams and he doesn't want to be on male teams because he's fearful of being outed and that it could be a pretty ugly situation. So I think that makes him less happy because sports have always been a very big part of her life, his life. One of the things I said to her when she told me about transitioning was that she was an awesome athlete that girl teams could use, so please don't do this. But it was what she wanted and he seems to be perfectly happy now with being identified as a male.

I've always been very, very proud of Nathan regardless of whether it's Natalie or Nathan. Young woman or young man, he's a wonderful person and he's got a lot to offer. I loved her then and I love him now and Nathan is going to make a contribution to humanity no matter what. I feel certain of that. So I'm okay with it. I love him unconditionally, but our relationship is a little strained and Nathan senses it too. Like I said, I have a hard time sticking to the pronoun. It doesn't come naturally to me. But I still want to hear about all of his friends and his classes and what he's doing and what his life is like, and how things are going for him. I still enjoy talking to him, but our relationship is different. Part of that is the difference between a relationship that a mother has with her daughter and the relationship that a mother has with her son.

Like when my daughters and I went shopping for wedding dresses, it never really dawned on us to include Nathan because we wouldn't have included my other son. I no longer treat her like one of the girls because now she's one of the guys. We don't do girl talk anymore. Nathan is obviously not interested and it's a little more difficult to share those kinds of things with him. We're still close, but not as close as we were when she was my daughter and definitely the type of closeness has changed. I think Nathan still tells me pretty much everything that's going on, but it's different. I have pictures of Nathan in my cubicle at work and when people ask me, because I'm new here, it was easy for me to just say that this is my son, Nathan. So it's not something that I have to tell people like I had a daughter, Natalie, but now I have a son called Nathan.

I raised four children by myself, worked two jobs, some cleaning toilets and that's no lie. I was very strong. All my kids knew that life is work, but it's what you make of it. I feel very lucky because what are the odds that a mother is going to have four children and they're all going to be such wonderful people. I do wish that I had stepped out on my own sooner and gotten them out of a really unhealthy situation. But one of my daughters told me that I never had to worry about her doing drugs—because she saw what happens and what they do and because they had an example that lived with them. My kids were probably street-wise, long before many adults, because of their biological father and when I think back, I did a good job. They saw a lot of things, but they're none the worse for the wear.

I wanted to be the kind of mother that they weren't afraid to come to and tell me anything because I loved them more than anyone else was ever going to love them. If they couldn't feel safe coming to me, then who in the world could they feel safe with? I wanted to be a part of their lives. I wanted to know who their friends and teachers were. I wanted to be more than just the person that provided dinner at the table every night. When I was raising my children, I thought it was important that they be independent and that didn't mean choosing the same lifestyle and making the same decisions that I had made. They're all separate people with separate lives. The fact that Nathan has chosen this lifestyle is his decision. When a child reaches a certain age, I think they know what's best for themselves and we, as parents, need to stand behind them and beside them and support them regardless, provided that they're not hurting someone else or themselves.

I was raised very devout. My dad was a Baptist preacher and I had religion shoved down my throat and so that was another thing that I always let my children choose. More people have died in the name of religion and God than for any other cause and I think that certain religions tend to create very narrow minds. When I think of mothers or family members who are unable to accept a lesbian daughter or a transgender child, I feel bad for them. I can't think of anything worse than to lose touch and closeness with a child simply because they can't accept their sexual preference or their lifestyle and what they do.

My own mother's style of mothering was very standoffish. I think that's one of the reasons that I was the kind of mom that I was. My mom was the kind of person that you tell what she wanted to hear, not what's real. I didn't want my kids to feel that way about me. I was an involved mom and was there all the time. My own mother was not that way. Granted, she too had four children and had to work, but she never came to my school plays. I missed one of my kid's school plays only because I was in the hospital giving birth to her brother. But I was sewing her bunny costume on the way to the hospital and had my ex-husband take it back home for her so she could have it for the school play the next day. That was the only school play I ever missed. I know my mom loves me and I love her, but it's not the same kind of love or closeness that I have with my daughters and I can honestly thank her because I knew what I didn't want to be like.

When Nathan came out to me as a lesbian, I was okay with it although I knew the hardships that were going to confront her. I don't know whether all transgenders come out as homosexuals first. But it didn't come as so much of a shock for me to see Nathan go from being a very dyke-ish lesbian to being a male. We're all entitled to live our lives the way that we best see fit. I learned a long time ago that life's too short not to make yourself happy. If you're not happy, then you need to change it and so, bottom line is, if that's what it takes for my child to be happy, then you go, boy, because that's what you need to do.

I would like to know what feelings trans people have that drive them to this decision and how it affects their lives. I do think it's genetic, a gene, a code that's hereditary. Nathan's grandfather came out as a homosexual although he was married to my ex-husband's mother for years and I can't imagine that their sex life was very good. I think that our family just passes along some gene. I do think there are rewards and positives just for having a transgender child. Nathan has certainly expanded our thinking and taught us new things. I don't know that I would be as open-minded if it weren't for him. If my son decided that he wanted to be a female, he'd be a cute one and I don't think my reaction would really be a whole lot different simply because of my belief that if it makes you happy, you need to do it. If she was a child or an adolescent, I don't know that I would have taken Nathan seriously. He might have had an easier time of it if I had been aware of his feelings and his desires at a younger age and I do think that I could have been more supportive.

I think that most people, our species, have a need to have permanent companionship. Nathan has not found this person and I'm hoping that eventually he will, even though he's not monogamous and has a hard time making commitments. He tells me about individuals that he's dating and I've found it very difficult that, as a male, he is homosexual and is attracted to homosexual men. It's kind of scary simply because of AIDS and I know that he's very promiscuous, always has been a very sexually-charged individual. I'm a little taken aback by the sudden change in orientation. I do know that he is still interested in women, so apparently he's bisexual. I can only hope that he's going to find someone that is truly going to make his life complete. But I don't expect that his life will be exactly as mine.

As a lesbian, she was still my daughter. As a transgender, she is no longer my daughter. She's my son. He's my son. But I really hated the thought of losing my daughter and the fact that I really enjoyed her. The changes that I've seen in Nathan have been kind of sad. I hope that as time goes by, he'll recapture his spirit because it seems to have deflated and left him. I think everybody's going to miss the same things that I am missing and the real sad thing will be is if his personality change remains the same.

I don't think that anyone would choose to put themselves through this sort of pain in terms of how other people look at you, or what other people think of you. I don't think that anyone would do it intentionally because they want to do something exciting, or that Nathan just woke up one day and said, "I think I want to be a guy." I think that there was a lot of inner turmoil about what people were going to think. What is my mother going to think? Is she still going to love me? To be honest, it's not that it's unacceptable, it's just that it's going to take time. Time makes everything better and I'm sure I have a lot more to go through before we're at the end of this road. It's been a year now since Nathan and I have actually spent any time together and I'm doing better with it. I'm truly looking forward to seeing him even though I know that it's going to be a difficult because it will be his first outing to our families. But I also have faith in my family and their love for Nathan.

Lisa, age forty-three, lived in Alaska. She was divorced and had plans to remarry. Lisa raised four children as a single mother and had worked at various jobs in order to support them. She graduated college around the time of the interview, majoring in archaeology. Lisa said she had no religious affiliation. Her child Natalie—now Nathan—disclosed as a lesbian at age seventeen and then told Lisa that he was planning to transition three years later in 1997. Although mostly attracted to gay men, Nathan identified as bi-sexual. Lisa called herself a feminist, was supportive of progressive and social justice movements, and although interested, had yet to attend a parents' group such as PFLAG. Lisa was interviewed by mail in 2001.

ADOLESCENCE

10
Debra

I FELT HELPLESS AS A MOTHER

WHEN JENNIFER WAS YOUNG, there were times when I did think maybe she was a lesbian. But I don't think I really knew although I had inklings over the years with different things that she had said or asked. But I didn't particularly have much concern about it. I did ask her why she didn't get as excited about boys as other girls did, but she didn't answer. We were so close her whole early childhood. Probably because she was an only child. We did everything together and I was just the happiest mom in the world. She was everything in my life.

Then at about thirteen, she turned into this monster teenager and I became her scapegoat. I guess for all the feelings she had that I didn't understand. She had a lot of problems as an adolescent. She was a good student, but not socially happy. She was depressed and she was ostracized a lot by her peers. She had weight problems. She was miserable. We were fighting and screaming all the time. I couldn't stand it. It just broke my heart. Most of our fights would be in the car and I got to a point that I thought there must be some kind of chemical thing in the car that was causing her to have some horrible toxic reaction the second she got in. I mean, she'd be banging and kicking the dashboard and screaming and totally disagreed with everything I ever said for two years. We would argue about what day of the week it was. I don't think it mattered. I didn't truly know what she was angry about and I would even intellectualize it and tell myself I should feel honored that she felt safe with me and able to do this because she knew my love was unconditional. But it hurt me so much that she was constantly despising me and everything I was.

Jennifer was about fourteen when she actually came out as a lesbian. She had a crush on a girl in her class who was her very best friend and she wrote her a letter. It was essentially a love letter and from what I understand, this girl was totally shocked and angry and repulsed by this letter and she showed it to her mother. Her whole class heard about this letter and so she was completely rejected and they wrote faggot on her locker and were hurtful in many ways that I'm sure she didn't always share with me. She was just trying to be brave and face it all herself without having the skills or any kind of gay support group. I don't think she knew any other gay kids. My fear was that people wouldn't understand and would ostracize her. That she'd be a social outcast because she was different and a lesbian unless she got herself to a place that was real diverse.

Then this girl's mother gave the letter to the principle who called me and just said, "Do you know your daughter's a lesbian?" Like it was a disease or something. There was a part of me that wanted to say, "Well duh. I know she's a lesbian and so what's your point? Why is that a problem?" But I think there was a part of me that was totally surprised to have it said and acknowledged. I guess he thought he was just informing me of why she was being treated this way at school. I feel like I pretty quickly understood and accepted it although I didn't know a lot about it. I wasn't very familiar with gay issues and I didn't have gay or lesbian friends that I knew of. I don't think I had terribly negative feelings. I thought this is how she feels. This is how she is. This isn't a stage. This is way too big to think that she couldn't know herself. I don't feel like I particularly grieved or felt sad about it. But it was also like a knife in my chest. I felt helpless as a mother. That I couldn't protect her from all the hurt in the world and people misunderstanding. I thought no one will know her the way I do and see all the good.

She had become so depressed and I really thought she could be suicidal. She never really made any attempt, but later on she told me that this boy at her school had said that he heard she tried to kill herself and that it was a shame she didn't succeed. Then her therapist called me up and said, "You know, kids kill themselves."

We talked about a psychiatric admission at an adolescent unit in a psychiatric hospital. She got hospitalized and she fully acknowledged that she was a lesbian to us in therapy sessions there and so this was an out issue now.

Her father and I differed a lot because he believed that she was too young to know and that she was experimenting and confused and what made her think she liked girls anyways. He thought she should try boys and take a guy out on a date and kiss him and go to the prom and see how it felt and maybe she could fall in love. To give it a shot. It made no sense at all. But afterwards she did move in with her father. I took her over and then I just completely isolated myself in my house and just watched sad movies and made myself cry all the time. I remember that it was a really good sobbing weekend that felt so therapeutic and was such a catharsis.

The other times I remember really big cries was when I would drive down to see her in the hospital. I would play Bette Midler singing *Baby Mine* and put it on repeat. The song was about a mother and all the hopes she had for her baby and, like me, all of the dreams and stuff for my child. How I wanted to protect her and didn't want anybody to ever hurt my baby and how they won't ever know her the way I do and see all the good in her. I wasn't crying especially because she was a lesbian, but because of her depression and the whole situation and her life. But actually, I also felt very happy to be on my own and away from the daily headaches of this kid who hated me and we got close again because she would come home occasionally on weekends. I didn't have to be in her face every day. So that was kind of ideal.

I didn't really have great difficulty telling people that she was a lesbian. I just quickly found a nice bunch of friends who were gay or lesbian and got involved and started learning about the issues and so now, seven years later, all my closest friends are gay or lesbian. I came out to people and because of her, my life changed direction and it's been the best thing. Once I got involved in the gay community, I became just totally proud and felt like an honorary lesbian and glad to have that identity. All the people I care about most seem to be gay or lesbian or transgender people.

I remember one time when she was about twenty. I was talking to her on the phone and saying, "What is it? What is wrong with you? I just don't understand. You have everything. You have a woman who loves you. A life partner that you're crazy about. You have a family who adores you. You have been to all the best schools. You have traveled. You are smart. People like you. You have friends now. What the hell is wrong with you? Why are you so miserable?" And she still couldn't say, "Don't you get it? This isn't even me." So, it sucked.

Then when she was twenty-two, she called me to say that she had something really important to talk to me about. We had dinner and afterwards went in the living room to talk. But right before she said it, I said it. "You want to have a sex change, don't you?" I guessed it and said it first. I didn't make her say it. She was stunned. Of course, you'd have to be blind not to know. It wasn't like out of the blue. She was always very butch. I asked her to explain and tell me more. I didn't get upset or cry or scream. He told me that as far back as he could remember, maybe three years old, he always knew he wanted to be a boy and that it was wrong and a mistake being a girl. He said that every birthday, when he blew out the candles on the birthday cake, he wished he could be a boy when he grew up. That was his wish on a cake. What a huge thing that is for a little kid! I felt like Super Mom because I really understood and gave her all of the positive support I could. I thought I was pretty special. Unusual in that I took it so well. We had the loveliest conversation.

As I said, there were always signs. I did know she wanted to be a boy as a very young child. She wanted everyone to call her Jimmy for several months and most of her friends were boys. When she was fourteen, she told me that she wished she was a boy and that someday she was going to grow up and be a man and have a sex change operation. I was really angry and said, "Well, you do that, but right now you're a girl. You're not a boy and you're not going to be a man. So get over it. Live with it." I made it clear that we're never discussing this again.

That's why puberty was hell for him. That's why getting his period and developing breasts and all these betrayals of his body made him hell to live with in early adolescence. No wonder she was depressed and suicidal. He was just furious and miserable. He, of course, learned to live with girl rules and the girl clothes and the girl expectations. He learned real quickly what was expected of a girl and he did it. But he never felt comfortable or happy. I never told her that she couldn't be a lesbian, but I told her she certainly couldn't be a boy. The poor kid was never a girl in her mind. What had I done that made her life so miserable that she couldn't be a girl? I was so unaware and it's so sad that I hadn't known. What kind of a mother was I?

A lesbian is nothing. This was really big. Who will understand? Parents of gay children who just learned their kid is gay feel basically upset because of who their child loves. Their child loves someone of the same sex and that's not what they anticipated and so they have to understand and adapt. I know that many parents are fearful of AIDS and violence if they have a gay son. I have more fears now than I did when she was a lesbian because of hate crimes and physical violence. But what I realized was that I was so sad because of who my child hated and that was herself. My child hated herself. Hated being her, hated being Jennifer, hated all the things that identified her to the whole world. He couldn't stand it. It was a mistake. What made me so terribly sad to realize was that it was such a horrible way to exist. No wonder she felt suicidal for so many years and was so despondent for years.

You see, Jennifer had to identify as a lesbian because she was in a female body and attracted to women. Later she told me that she never felt like a lesbian. That she didn't feel like she belonged in the lesbian community because she always knew she was really male and would eventually transition. I had sometimes wondered why she didn't embrace all of the gay and lesbian stuff that there was, like pride events. I gave her lesbian jewelry and she wouldn't wear them. It's just that she never was proud to be a lesbian because she never felt like she was. She always felt like she was male. But of course, she was a minor and she was in a female body. So that's how she had to identify. But I didn't realize it at the time. Now looking back, I think of all the things that I expected her to do as a young woman. Like getting dressed up. I made her wear a dress once. It must have been horrible for her. Humiliating. But I didn't know she didn't think she was female, that she identified as male. I once said, "Tough. I don't care if you're a lesbian. You can still wear a nice skirt." I just thought she was such a dyke that she didn't like dresses.

So I was Super Mom. At least for the first few months. What I wanted was to figure out how I could be the most supportive mother and learn as much as I could. I rarely allowed myself to feel what it felt like, and what I missed and what sorrow I had. But I had to grieve and let go of my daughter and accept it. I was the mother of a son. Jennifer was now Joshua. I had to stop saying *she* and *her* and start using the right pronouns and his new name. I had to grieve because I thought all these years that I had a daughter and I realized that I didn't and never really did. It all felt so bogus. It felt like it was all a lie. Like I was duped. I didn't really know my own child. I felt so close to her. How could I not realize such an intimate important thing about his whole life and feel so close to this child and not even know this? What kind of mother was I?

So I questioned our closeness and how much I really knew my kid. I thought she was a happy kid. Once I said to her, "I remember times you were such a happy little girl and such a happy baby and we had such good times." He said, "Sure. Of course, I have wonderful, happy memories, but this was always there." It did explain so much. But this was huge. I was in a really awful depression. I felt so isolated by this because I couldn't talk to anyone about it. I didn't know where to take it. Who in the hell could understand this? I felt so sad that my little girl was gone and all the things I had thought were a hoax. A lie.

I was so depressed, feeling like I hadn't known and what kind of bad mother was I—and also, I'm losing my little girl and who's going to understand this. I started going to a therapist and she thought it would be good for me to look at baby pictures and gather all my thoughts in a basket and dwell on memories of childhood things and then set it aside. Kind of let it go, to move on. I felt afraid to do that. I didn't want to lose her. I didn't want to stop saying I have a daughter. I wasn't ready to have her be a different person even though he told me that he was still the same inside. That we still share all the same memories and the same values and tried to reassure me that he wasn't really changing. It was just outwardly and how he was perceived by other people and his name. That he was really the same. But I had to learn to see him in a totally different way. She was gone.

It was like I was totally losing her. I felt like I was grieving because I was losing my daughter, but it's not the kind of grief that anyone can recognize. I was still not ready or comfortable just telling everyone and you don't get flowers and casseroles like you do with a death. But my daughter is gone. She's died. She's not there anymore and so I have to learn to know a whole new person. I felt such a separation from her. A true loss of this girl who had grown up to be a woman that I treasured. It made me realize that all the little things I imagined, all the dreams I had were mostly for her happiness. All I really wanted was for my baby and my little girl and my child to grow up—as every parent does—to be healthy and happy. It killed me to realize that he was living with so much pain for so many years and kept it from me because he didn't want to hurt me. Because I couldn't fix it. I felt pretty helpless and sad. So sad to realize that he had been carrying this burden around without me knowing for so many years. I felt responsible for not making it easy enough for him to tell me.

It took three months for me to start to talk about it. I didn't tell a lot of people. As a parent, I had to come out too. I guess I feared how I would be treated, but for the most part it went well. I called the International Foundation for Gender Education and I called a club in the area and I got magazines and articles and I learned as much as I could. Then I started meeting people in transition, trying to get totally up to speed with what this experience is about. All I thought about was how I can be the best supportive person and what can I learn. I started going to PFLAG. I joined pretty quickly after she told me about her plans for transition.

Joshua is having the top surgery done in two weeks. He is excited as can be and so happy and thrilled to have his breasts basically removed and able to pass more easily as a male. Just to wear a T-shirt without horrible binders and corsets and things underneath and be comfortable in the summer. He's looked forward to this for years. I'm excited for him. I'm totally, totally thrilled. I got him the name of the surgeon and when I talk to him on the phone, he's just so much happier although he's fearful because he's overweight and it's more risk. I don't like five hours of anesthesia, being a nurse and knowing the things that could happen. But I can't say that I feel terribly worried. Joshua would very much like to have genital surgery, but the options aren't too good and it's so complicated and difficult and painful with multiple steps and the outcome is still so unsatisfactory that it's much easier to go from male to female. It's just easier to dig a hole than to build a pole. I mean it's easier surgically to change from a male to a female. I know that his father really sees it as a terrible tragedy and a mutilation which is horrific. He took about two and a half years to tell his wife and he still really can't deal with it. He doesn't want to call him Joshua.

Joshua could be an XY chromosome and not even meant to be female. We talked about it and he wanted to be tested a year or two ago, but wondered what would he do with the information anyway. He thought he might be disappointed if he really was XX, meaning that he was actually biologically female. I guess I don't know how I explain it or make sense of it except that I totally respect that a person just knows from early on in their lives who and what they are. I guess there were times when I briefly wondered what could have happened that might have caused it, but I can't say that I cared too much. I don't think I've looked for any medical explanation.

When I was at PFLAG, I could feel the transition in my own head happen as I went to meetings. I was never uncomfortable talking about it. But it was so foreign to think of having a son. I always would say I have a daughter who lives with a girlfriend and she recently told me that she feels that she needs to transition into a male. So I have a transsexual child and her name is Joshua. It took a while and then it was such a cool feeling to finally get to a meeting where I remember everybody applauded the first time when I said, "I have a son who lives with his girlfriend." Some new people looked at me like, "Okay. Where's the problem? What are you doing here? You have a straight son." And then I was just able to say it. Actually some of my difficulty was in recognizing that I was happy about what was going on in spite of it causing a great deal of pain for my child. There's so much to go through still that's going to be pretty difficult, but I'm happy that he could tell me and move on. I feel very comfortable and love PFLAG. I feel like it's family. I care about everybody there and like them all. I feel very welcome and accepted. I don't feel ostracized, but I am still totally different and alone. From time to time there are other transgender people that come to meetings, or parents of these kids. But I feel pretty different in that they can't really relate.

My partner is trans. Since I met him, it's never been difficult at all for me to see him as male and I see him as my boyfriend. I don't think of him as a male who used to be a female. I know that's true, but I don't see him that way. But people who I've told, they sort of think that I'm a lesbian. Because people think that he's female until he gets a penis. That's what makes you a male when you get that operation, and until then, don't be trying to pass as a male. That's what people seem to think. But it's not true. It's all in your head. It's all about who you are. Who you feel you are and how you express yourself.

I think gay people have a lot of trouble with transgendered people and don't feel that inclusion with us at all. I don't like having to feel left out and resentful of the gay community. I think we're the bastards of the movement. One's gender and the other is sexual orientation. Totally different things, but they have so much in common that we could benefit by working together. I know a lot of lesbians feel totally betrayed and kind of insulted that a lesbian would say, "I'm a man, I wasn't just a butch lesbian. I've always been a man." Because people assume that dykes that are especially butch really want to be men. It isn't true. They know they are female and that they love women and it's just how they express themselves. It's insulting for people to assume they really want to be men so when one of them leaves the fold, and does it and becomes a man, that's just like insulting.

Debra , age fifty-two, was divorced and worked as a nurse. She identified herself as Unitarian and was in a relationship with a FTM trans man. Her one child Jennifer—now Joshua—came out as a lesbian at age fourteen and began planning transition at age twenty-two in 1998. Debra was a trans activist and a representative to PFLAG from a local transgender group. Her political interests included abortion rights, ERA, civil rights and the environment. She lived in Connecticut and was interviewed in 2000.

11
Rina

MOM, THAT'S ME, I AM A BOY, INSIDE I AM A BOY

FROM THE BEGINNING, HE, MY SON JACK, was different. When he started school at five, he didn't want to go. He would fight me, screaming and yelling, as I dragged him to the car morning after morning. After a year of this, I asked him, "Why is it? Just tell me why you don't want to go to school? What is it at school that is so horrible?" He said, "Nothing is horrible." But he didn't see why he had to wear a dress when the other boys wore shorts. He would come up with reasons for not wearing a dress. That it hurt when he sat down. It was too tight round his neck. He couldn't climb trees. People could see his underpants and he got colds because the wind blew up it. I said, "Darling, that's the way girls dress for school." He said, "But the other boys don't." So I said if he wanted, he could buy a boy's school uniform. So he did. At six years old, he marched into a shop and bought himself a pair of shorts and a shirt. He wore them every day and I washed them every day.

I heard other mothers refer to me as the mother who dressed her child as a boy. But I never let it worry me too much. He was happy at school. His teacher was amused by it. Everybody was amused by it. I just thought that he was a feminist, very interesting and intelligent. My husband and I, well, we just thought of him as a tomboy. It was only later that he told us how confusing that was for him because he thought being a tomboy was just a type of boy. For four years he wore a boy's uniform to school. Then a new principal arrived and said he couldn't be in the school choir because he was not wearing the correct uniform. That was fine because he couldn't sing anyway. Then he couldn't be in the school photograph, but his teacher snuck him in at the last minute so we do have a photograph of him in a boy's uniform. Then the same principal said that he couldn't be in the advanced math class because he was making himself too different from the rest of the kids. That we were furious about so we changed to a Montessori school. They didn't have uniforms and he could wear what he liked until high school—which in Australia is age twelve. Then girls were required to wear skirts so I sewed them into culottes which was fine with him. And that was that. Later, after he transitioned, he was allowed to use the principal's toilet and to wear the boy's school uniform which he did.

I think he was very happy during his last year at school. Oh, there were some incidents. A group of boys ambushed him one day and said, "Hey, are you a boy or a girl?" And he turned round and said, "Yes." But I knew he hid in the library and didn't have many friends. The friends he did have, we used to laugh, because we'd call them the misfits. Two of his friends were gay boys. He had a friend who was particularly fat that nobody else was friends with. He gathered around him those people who had nobody else.

He was fifteen when he came upon a program called *The Wrong Body* and he called me to watch it with him. Now, just before that he'd been stage manager of a play and was obviously infatuated with one of the girl actors. I thought, my goodness, he's a lesbian. I thought about how he was into *Star Wars* and all boy type things and I thought, "Okay, she's a lesbian." So I was ready. I was ready for lesbian and I prepared a speech that said, "I love you. This isn't quite what I've chosen for you, but if it makes you happy, this is fine. I still love you and I always will." It didn't worry me. But then we watched *The Wrong Body*, and he said to me, "Mom, that's me. I am a boy. Inside I am a boy exactly like that person on the program." I didn't know what to say, I was so taken aback. So I used exactly the speech I had prepared for a lesbian.

I spent that entire night on the Internet trying to find out about transgendered and transsexual people, what the difference was, what it meant, and what the possibilities were. There was nothing Australian. Nothing at all. All American stuff. But I did find a list for an Australian group and I wrote to them saying, "If there's anybody out there, help me, please." Two people answered back. A woman and a guy from England. For the next few months, I corresponded with both of these people and they helped me enormously.

For the first month Jack would not tell his father. I kept telling him, "Tell your dad. Please tell your dad." He wanted me to tell him, but I didn't want his dad to blame me or to say that I'd encouraged him. My husband, Ron, always told me that I allowed this child to do anything she wanted. So it had to be Jack that told him. In the end he did and Ron took the next day off and read everything that I had saved on the computer about transgender. He was totally supportive and has been ever since. We told our other children and made James, the youngest, our pronoun boy. He was the one who had to correct us every time we said the wrong pronoun. We were saying *he* and *his* from then on and every time we got it wrong, James' job was to correct us. It was great fun for a ten-year-old to correct his parents. But it was an awful year. A dreadful year. I thought if I got through that year, I could get through anything. It was just like grief. Losing, losing a daughter, although Jack said that I wasn't. That he hadn't changed.

I had to tell people. My parents, we told, and my brother and my sisters. The sister I was closest to accepted it, but her husband didn't and they didn't let their sons see Jack for two years. I don't know what they were afraid of. That their boys would catch something from him. The person I thought would give me the most support was my brother, but his reaction was the worst of my whole family. He said, "He'll pass as a boy, but he'll never be a man and I'd rather have ill children that were going to die than have a child like Jack." I was in tears. He's never apologized for that, but he's accepted Jack and he tries his best to use the male pronoun. But that first year was dreadful.

My father was a minister and it was very, very difficult for him and for my mother. I think they prayed about it for a long time. Then another pastor said to them, "That poor boy. Just imagine. You think what you're going through. What his parents are going through. But imagine what he's been through all his life." I think that opened my mother's eyes and she began to think of it a different way. I told all my friends. I would say, "You're going to have to know anyway and I'd rather you'd hear from me and ask any questions that you've got rather than talk about it behind my back and get the facts wrong." They were all just great.

Other people we told as they needed to know. People who'd known Jack as a child. They'd ask how were my children, and then I'd tell them. I figured if I was calm and cool about it, they would just follow my lead. I'd say that "Jack has been diagnosed as transgendered which means that inside he has always been a boy and he's going to transition. So when you see him, you'll probably notice a difference. He's going to appear as a male." And he did. He'd had his hair cut very short. He looked like a boy. He was passing as a boy. Now everybody who needs to know knows. Occasionally I will meet people who I haven't seen since my children were little and I'll have to say something. But it's so rare now that I have to tell anybody.

Like lots of transgender people, he used to bind and he was just in agony those Australian summers. He'd get such bad rashes that he'd bleed. But he'd still do it. It was just dreadful for him. I just felt so sorry for him. He wanted to have top surgery, but in New South Wales they don't allow anybody under eighteen to have top surgery. But in Queensland, north of New South Wales, the law allows it if it comes under cosmetic surgery, and if the parents give permission. But the cosmetic surgery needs to be for medical reasons so my family doctor suggested that we see a psychiatrist who would test him for gender dysphoria. I said to Jack, "What if they say you're not. What if we go through months of psychiatrists and they say that you're not gender dysphoric?" Jack said, "Well, it really won't matter because I won't be around. I'll be sure I'm gone after that." He virtually told me that if he couldn't live as a guy, he would commit suicide and I was not willing to have a dead child. There was no way I would not fight for him. So then came the horrendous job of going to psychiatrists. And I went with him all the time and we got through it.

The first psychiatrist was great. We had to show that, as a child, Jack never wanted to be a girl. Never even thought of himself as a girl. We took along the school photographs where he had been dressed as a boy from first to fourth class. But then we had to have a second opinion which was horrible. The second psychiatrist told

Jack that he was probably a lesbian and that what he wanted to do was just sleep with girls. And if that's what he wanted, then this wasn't the way to go about it. He said, "If you want to sleep with girls, have sex with girls, that makes you a lesbian. Doesn't it?" Jack said, "No." And the doctor said, "Well, what do you think it makes you?" And Jack said, "A boy." He made Jack cry and I got really upset, but I wasn't allowed to speak. It made me so angry, but it was just a test. It was just a test to diagnose him.

Well, anyway, all the psychiatrists had this meeting and they decided that Jack was gender dysphoric and there was absolutely nothing else wrong with him. They actually congratulated us in bringing up such a well-balanced child. So he got his papers that said he was gender dysphoric and the psychiatrists were willing to say that he could have cosmetic surgery for medical reasons and that it would substantially improve the quality of his life. Jack was really so excited about this and I couldn't see him binding anymore, it was just so dreadful. So he had his top surgery and we did the name change. Actually, he changed his name before he was sixteen.

He'd been on testosterone injections for around nine months after his diagnosis and he was so pleased that his periods had stopped. Then we learned about this new program in Australia where you can have hormone implants. Usually it's for males that have low testosterone counts, but they wanted to see whether it would work with transgendered people. If Jack was willing and if I signed, because he was still under eighteen, he could be a candidate. We had planned to go overseas at the end of high school, but he couldn't get the injections overseas so we agreed to have an implant to see how it worked and he's been on implants ever since. Every six months. They work terrifically and that's his testosterone.

Best of all, I was able to get him a British passport with male on it because I'm British, which he couldn't do in Australia. You can change your passport in Britain, but you can never change your birth certificate because it's an historical document. Then he got his driver's license after he got a British passport. So his driver's license says male and he was able to enroll in college and get a job as a male. But he can never marry in Australia. And the way our adoption laws are, he can't adopt a partner's children. The other thing is that in order to get a visa to go to America, he'd have to sign a form saying that he'd been diagnosed with a psychiatric disorder because transgender is still a psychiatric disorder. So he'd have to lie if he didn't want to publicize it. He'd have to lie if he wanted to go to America.

His Australian passport still has female on it and still will until he has surgery. A hysterectomy or something like that. That's when you can change your sex on your birth certificate and passport in Australia. I'd like to change the Australian law that says you have to have a hysterectomy before you can change your birth certificate—because you can't change the gender on your passport unless you've changed the gender on your birth certificate. That's the way the Australian law is at the moment. But if Jack had a hysterectomy, it's very likely that his fallopian tubes would wither away and they are now using fallopian tubes to construct a penis. He doesn't want to have a hysterectomy because he doesn't want to ruin his chances of having the best possible phalloplastic surgery later on. He is not interested at the moment simply because the surgery is not good enough. He doesn't want to wreck his life and ruin his chances of sexual feeling and all the rest of it simply by having an operation. Anyways, we can't afford it.

Jack is lucky because I'm a British citizen, but all the rest of transgendered people in Australia are stuck with having a passport in their original gender. That's extraordinarily embarrassing, so they tend not to travel. I would like to see medical science improve enormously and very quickly and let us be able to include surgery overseas in our medical benefits. That would be really nice. Mostly, I would like to see people accepted for what they are, really more than anything. I'd like to help some of the mothers get over what they are going through. Some are having these enormous guilt trips. What did I do to make my child this way, and all the rest of it. They shouldn't have to go through that. I would like so much to make things easier for Jack obviously. As a mother, isn't that what one would want to do? Make things easier for their child.

I cried. I did cry. I still have his ponytail that he cut off. But he doesn't know that. I changed all the phony photographs on the wall. I took down the ones with long hair where he looked like a girl so that when he brings his friends over, it just looks like he's been a boy all his life. I went through all of our family photos and picked out the ones where he looks most like a boy and those are the ones that went up on the wall and we went out and had a family photo taken with Jack looking very, very masculine. His main problem isn't that he's transgendered. His main problem is his height. He's only five feet and one inch tall, which is very short for a guy. I think that's his major worry. That he's so short. He looks very young by the way.

He's now nearly twenty. I can't think of him as a girl anymore. He never really was. I'm used to calling him my son. But he doesn't tell people or friends at work that he's transgendered. And he doesn't want to be involved in transgender activism. Actually, I would like to so much make it easier for him to tell people. I don't think that he would hide it, if it came out. I think he would just say, "That's me. Not a problem." And he would expect that people wouldn't have a problem with it and maybe they wouldn't because he's just a great person.

Interestingly enough, his relationships are with both males and females and he does relate really well to the young gay crowd who are fabulous kids. Lovely, lovely people and my house is now full of young gay boys. But his relationships have been with both boys and girls and I'm happy with that. He's always prized the person over the package and I think that's a great lesson that he's teaching other people too. That it doesn't matter what you look like on the outside. It's who you are inside.

The most problematic thing for Jack in the future is going to be his relationships. That's going to be a problem and I worry. There was one time he wanted to ask one of the women at work out, but he didn't. The reason was because he'd have to tell her and if it didn't work out, she might tell everyone. I worry and I don't mean to be crude, but gay boys are so concerned about the size of their accouterments. Poor Jack. I don't know how he copes with that. I don't ask. I do think he's definitely bisexual. Sometimes I think he goes more toward the gay boys, but he also takes women out. It doesn't bother me. I really don't want to know the intricacies of his love life. I just want him to be happy and he seems to have lots of good friends. One day he'll find somebody to love him who will love him for what he is, and that's all that matters. He does talk to me when I push it, but we have to be in a certain frame of mind and he has to be willing to talk. It seems all so private and personal, but I guess if he needs to talk about it, I'm the only person he could talk to. I have said to him to be careful, to be safe.

I was a non-sexist child raiser. That's what I believed in. My own mother's style of mothering was very traditional. But I was never a traditional girl. I was a tomboy. I was very outspoken. I was encouraged to be intelligent, to search out my own answers, and to state my mind. I think my mother was pleased with me when I did that actually. Although she brought me up to be a lady, I would never use that word for myself now. But she also brought me up to be a very strong woman, and that's what I am, I guess. She was always busy so she left me alone a lot of the time. I think that was a good thing. It taught me to be self-sufficient at a very early age. I look back and I'm pleased with that. There were a couple of things that my parents did that I still think were wrong. But it had to do with their religion, not anything else. I still believe there's a God, but I don't believe that God makes rubbish. I think that God created Jack the way he is. That's all.

I wanted to be the kind of mother who loved my kids. Who brought them up to be the best they could be. To let them be themselves. I really didn't put many restrictions on them. I did want them to do their schoolwork. I wanted them to make that a priority. After that, I let them do whatever they wanted to as long as it didn't hurt them or hurt somebody else. I think my own mother thought, at least for a while, that Jack was my fault. But being a male inside wasn't in any way a reflection of how I brought him up. It made it easier for him. I really truly believe that. It wasn't a question of fault or guilt. Well, maybe at first. What causes this, and could it possibly be that I was worried when I was pregnant with him? You know, high testosterone levels caused by stress. Those types of things did go through my mind. I tried to do some research to find out. But if it did affect him, so what. I mean you still have to live with the child. I've done the best I can and I certainly wouldn't have done it on purpose. Unfortunately, he was born into the wrong body.

Looking back, I would have to ask how could I have been so blind? How could I have not known? I really should have known much, much earlier. I should have been the one who picked up on it. If it had been a boy dressing up in little girl's clothes, I would have picked up on it much, much earlier. At least there would be more information on it. Sometimes I think if I'd had a son who transitioned to female, at least I would be able to go shopping with him for clothes. I would love that. We could have had great fun. A glorious time. I do shop with Jack, but the clothes he buys are such boring clothes. But because Jack was in a female body dressing up as a male, it was much more difficult to pick up on. Because we've got words like tomboy. Jack has never been a girl. Never, never been feminine. Ron and I used to say that he walked like an elephant. No, I should have picked it out much earlier. It was a surprise. It was a shock. But looking back, I'd say to myself, it's my fault it's a surprise. I should have known.

I really like the gay scene. I mean I have been friends with gay men all my life. From the time that my children were little, I've had foreign exchange students in the house. My whole idea was to show them that everybody is an individual and you accept people for what they are and not based on stereotypes. That has always been what I have taught my children. They have grown up with that. I guess that's made their acceptance of Jack and Jack's acceptance of himself so much easier. We accept transgender people as normal people. They are normal people.

A lot of people reject their children and a lot of their children are kicked out of home and trying to find their own way of making their money on the street. I feel so sorry for them. I think the parents are wrong. They're not being fair to their children. Maybe it's personality characteristics. Like intolerance. Like ignorance or lack of information. Or fear maybe. The way they've been brought up perhaps. Maybe lack of love. If you can't accept somebody, you can't say you love them. You should love your children irrespective. For the person they are. You can't say I'd love you if you were different. Lesbian or gay means nothing for goodness sake. It is so incredibly minor. Who cares? If my children told me they were lesbian or gay, I'd say fine and where are you going tonight and have you done your homework? It's just such a minor thing. I really cannot understand that people make big fusses about it. Transgendered people have to go through so much more.

I want people to be able to accept. I want people to understand that it doesn't matter who you are, or what you are. You're perfect just being a human being. I hope I've taught my own children that. Why would somebody wish to change their gender? That is their gender. It's their body that's wrong. Why would they wish to change it? Nobody would wish to put themselves through what transgendered people put themselves through. It's not a case of wishing. It's a case of imperative. That's the way they are inside and they need to express what they are. When I really think about it, I've got a theory that it's like sexuality in the sense of the continuum business. Some people are totally gay. Some people are totally straight and there are all sorts of people, most of us, in-between. I think maybe gender is similar. Some people are totally male and some people are totally female and there are all sorts of people in between. I'm an extraordinarily strong woman. Maybe I would be at the feminine end. But there's nothing feminine about me actually. I dress in dresses, but I don't think of myself as pretty or feminine.

But there are some people who cross over that middle line in the sense that although their bodies are female or their bodies male, they are so, so far male in a female body—or female in a male body that their bodies become a problem to them. They can't express themselves in the body that they find themselves in. If you think of it that way, it really makes sense. So, let them change their bodies. People have nose jobs because they don't like their noses. Why not just let people change their bodies so that they're happy with them. I mean, it would be so much easier wouldn't it? If we just accepted. If we just took people the way they are and said, "OK, do it. Do whatever you have to make yourselves content and happy in this world."

It was hell for Jack before he knew what was wrong with him. He always knew that he felt like a boy and when he saw that program, everything just sort of fell into place. He is by far the easiest of all my children to get along with. We're very close. He and I have come through a lot together. I've been his support. I know that's the case and I know that he's grateful for that. He's a great person. He's my friend and I wouldn't be able to get by without him. I enjoy having him as a son. I loved him before. I love him now I'm so pleased that he's happy now. I think it's wonderful that he feels so good. He's doing great things with his life. He's got a lovely crowd of friends. I'm proud of him and I couldn't hope to have a better child.

I've had my tears. But they're over. I don't cry now. I'm happy for him now. I hate to think of what would have happened if he couldn't have told me when he did. Jack has been through minimum trauma. Okay, so he had a few more hassles than the other children have had. But that was my job, to minimize the trauma. I think I did that well. I'm sure I did that well. I minimized his hassles, smoothed his way, and made his life as easy as I could. That's a mother's job anyway. That's part of what you become a mother for.

Rina, age forty-seven, was born in England and lived in Australia. She was married and had worked as a teacher. Rina had three children and said that she had no particular religious affiliation. Her child Jack began to transition at age fifteen in 1996 and identified as bisexual. Rina was active in progressive and social justice movements such as feminism, civil rights, the peace movement, and the environment. She belonged to PFLAG and was an activist in the transgender civil rights movement as well as in her local gay and trans communities. Rina was interviewed by mail in 2001.

12

Beth

I JUST DON'T LIKE LABELS

OFFICIALLY, I SAY OFFICIAL BECAUSE I think I knew before Nikki told me. She was around sixteen and was working at this camp, a type of a church place. She told me that something happened and she was pretty upset. She was part of this counselor group that was very tight and close and some of the people said that they thought that she was in a relationship with this other girl and that she should sort of fess up and come clean in the group that she was gay. My daughter was upset because she didn't agree and she didn't like them labeling her.

Nikki was just so confused. She told me that she wasn't sure, that she didn't really know. So that's how it began. I was irritated at the people who were labeling her before she was ready to be labeled. I actually get irritated at any labeling. My own philosophy is that calling people gay or lesbian is misleading. I think that sexuality is a continuum and there are some times in people's lives when they would rather be with males, or with females—or maybe more with females. I just don't like labels in general and I certainly didn't like that my daughter was being labeled before she really knew. Now as I look back, they probably saw something that maybe she didn't even see herself—or wasn't ready to see. So that's how it first came up.

The issue for me was, is she or isn't she? She did describe some of the things she would do with this friend. They would go off a lot and take walks and hold hands sometimes and sometimes hug and sometimes kiss and things like that. When I heard this, I thought that she must be coming to terms with some part of her sexuality and I just felt like this is going to be a big thing for us all. I mean adjusting and it's not going to be an easy road in life for her because of society.

So that was the beginning. I think it might have been a couple of weeks, or maybe a month after that when we were out camping and she said, "I think I'm in love." And I said, "That's great. I'm glad you're in love." Then she said, "I think I'm in love with Alicia." I looked at her and I said, "Oh." And then she looked at me and said, "You're not saying that's great, you know." I just couldn't at that time and looking back, I feel pretty badly that I wasn't there yet. I just wasn't there for her. She's so perceptive and she called me on it right away. I think I remember saying, "Are you sure?" Or something like that instead of telling her that it was wonderful that she was in love. Maybe I said it was great, but not with much feeling.

I think I felt a little overwhelmed. I can't remember how I felt. I think I felt, "Oh my God! What's she going to do? What are we going to do?" Because it's not the norm. Not normal. I just remember feeling a little numb. Kind of like everything was a blur. It was an emotionally hard moment for me and I'm sure it was for her. What hurts me the most, and I can almost cry about it now, because she was so excited and I just couldn't be there for her. She was so happy and so excited that she was in love. But maybe I'm too hard on myself.

I can't believe I can't remember if she told her father. I must be blanking on what happened. I think she might have asked me to tell him, but I'm not certain because she was extremely open and close with him. They're very tight. Whether she told him or I told him, I can't remember. But he really didn't have much of a problem with it. I have some colleagues who are gay. I have some gay friends that I sing with in a singing group. I've acted in a lot of theater. I think I'm so open to a lot of things, but I just wasn't ready for this.

I did tell my mother. She was the only person that I told for a while and it was surprisingly great. My mother kind of looks and acts a little bit like Edith on *All in the Family*. So I told her that Nikki has this girlfriend, and she said, "Oh, that's nice. I'm glad she has a girlfriend." It was kind of funny. I said, "No Mom, a girlfriend." And then she said, "That's great and Nikki's a great person." She was very accepting.

I should have known. She didn't like to dress up. She wanted a bike that she could do stunts on. When she was about eleven or twelve, she had a big crisis with this neighborhood friend and began having nightmares. I was concerned and we brought her to a therapist. They only met about three or four times and we had a couple of family sessions. I was wondering if she was struggling with her sexuality and I asked the therapist if he thought maybe she was gay. That I had this feeling. He looked at me and said, "I don't think so. Where are you getting this from? Are you projecting?" And because of that therapist, I just kind of let it go.

Well, after she told me, I gave her a lot of information that I got from PFLAG and we both went to this gay youth conference. She was so funny. She asked me to hold her hand so they would think we were a couple. I did walk in with her and stayed a little bit because professionally, I wanted to get some information. Then I left and she stayed there by herself. I was so proud of her. Afterwards, I found her the name of a gay youth group close by and she went there one night with one of her friends. So she has support from the gay youth community—and from us anytime she needs to talk. Especially about relationships. Sometimes I want to talk about what's going on with her and her sexuality, but I don't know where to start. I want to ask her how she's doing. How she's feeling. If she has enough people to talk to. But I'm afraid to put her in too much of a box because the big thing is she really doesn't want to be labeled. She just wants to be.

She's just been blossoming this last year at high school. She cut her hair real short. She actually started a diversity club there even though there's not much diversity. She's an artistic and sensitive person. She plays guitar and sings and writes songs and poetry. She's very funny. She got voted class clown. Charismatic. She's my baby and she's a great kid. I was concerned that she would get depressed because she had been depressed before, but it didn't happen. Sometime I wonder if she has enough people to talk to, or to be with. She did try to go to a queer prom once, but didn't because she was sick. But she also has mentioned that she thinks she might be bisexual and sometimes she talks about a hot guy.

So it still may be unclear to her. She doesn't tell a lot of people. Only close friends. Actually, she has more straight friends so she doesn't have that core identity type of a thing. When she's with her straight friends, she'll talk about the hot guys. Maybe it's to fit in. But I know that she still loves Alicia who is not in the picture anymore, so it's very difficult for her. She's been holding on to that relationship for a long time. I have been worried about people talking about her or ostracizing her, but for the most part, it hasn't really played out.

She's going to college in California and she doesn't seem to be concerned about people there knowing she's gay. I mean there are a lot of gays and lesbians at the college so she's going to have a lot of support. She's going to come into her own, whatever that is. Bisexual or whatever. I think that she's still kind of exploring her sexuality. I don't think that she's one hundred percent sure if she's gay. I think that the generation she's part of is a lot more accepting. My older daughter was great. She said that being gay was a cool thing.

I guess my philosophy is that a mother should do as much as possible for their children. Especially to try to understand and be open to listening. That's what I try to do and I can get into that mode the easiest when I'm not fearful or worried myself. I do think I've done pretty well with it. I do wish I were more accepting of parents that can't accept a gay child. To put aside their fears and feelings of right and wrong. But some people just can't do that. I've been in touch with this legislator about an upcoming co-parent adoption bill. He told me that it wasn't right. That he wasn't brought up that way. I guess it's a homophobic thing. A fear thing. Maybe afraid of his own feelings. Maybe some parents are so insecure that they don't want to be ostracized or shamed. I don't think they're bad people. I just think that they want to sweep it under the rug.

I have a suspicion that one of my nephews might be gay and he comes from a very, extremely religious situation. My sister actually converted to Catholicism and she has these right and wrong beliefs. I really don't think she wants to know. I did tell her about Nikki, but I don't think she told her husband and her reaction was that it probably was a phase. My heart goes out to her son.

He still lives at home and doesn't go anywhere. It upsets me very much. I've read about families who just throw them out. I could almost see my brother-in-law doing something like that. It's just going to be hard for my daughter and because I'm a mother, it's going to be hard for me—knowing it's going to be hard for her in life. She won't be able to participate fully in society. And there are hurtful people. I just want her to find what's right for herself. But I don't see her as a conforming type young woman anyway.

My husband and I just came back from Provincetown and we saw so many couples that were so happy. So free! Walking arm in arm and it was great! Celebrating who they are. There are some neat parts of being gay. You can work toward a cause like lesbian rights. You can have a family. It's just so encouraging to see the changes like civil unions in Vermont. Changes like that, even if they happen slowly, make me hopeful.

Beth, age fifty, was married and worked as a mental health counselor. She had two children. Her youngest daughter, Nikki, began to question her sexual orientation at age sixteen in 1998. Beth identified herself as a feminist and was active in town politics. She lived in Connecticut and was interviewed in 2000.

NOT THE ONLY ISSUE

13
Lila

I REGRET THE KIND OF MOTHER I WAS

I'VE BEEN REALLY UNCERTAIN ABOUT BEING interviewed although I was curious about your study and what you expected to find. You see, the issue, my issue, isn't about my daughter Marci being a lesbian. Not really. Of course, I worry about her safety and I was disappointed. Grandchildren. I would have liked grandchildren, I guess. And of course, I've wondered why. I mean the effect of family and all that. But let me tell you how she told me.

I had wondered for a time. Not wondered. I really knew. Maybe for about two years. She was dressing, well, more and more butchy. She was calling herself a radical feminist and going around saying how she lived in this women's community. That she told me. She also was referring to different women friends, telling me they were lesbians, and bringing along all these books on lesbianism the times when she came back home. Maybe she was preparing me. I could have asked, but she was always so much on the defensive. I've always been a bit wary, kind of afraid of her. Her rudeness. Her temper. Oppositional. And we weren't seeing that much of each other anyways. At eighteen, she left for college and never really lived at home after that. I would have to be the one who called her. She rarely called me. Mostly when she needed something. Everything was an argument. Like we were meant to disappoint each other.

I always knew a lot of gay people from living in New York City. Faculty at my college and also lots of students in my old department. And because I've been involved in theater. I did have more than one affair with different women when I was young. But I never thought of myself as a lesbian. I was living in the Village back then and was kind of what they called a beatnik. During the '50s, well it was the cool thing to do, at least in the Village. As long as you slept with men too. Maybe I could have been gay, but those times were not all that easy and I wanted a good life. And that meant marriage and children. My parents were very conventional and really over-concerned about what other people thought. They probably would have rejected me totally. So, I guess I was bisexual enough or lucky enough to have a choice. And no, it wasn't any unconscious thing I wished on my daughter. Some psychiatrist I was seeing at the time suggested that maybe I wanted my daughter to live the life I couldn't—and that was the end of analysis with him. I do think perhaps it's genetic, or maybe it has something to do with the times. I mean so many young women coming out. If I were her age now, maybe it could have been me.

She moved to California right after college and then came home to visit with a friend. This was two years ago. Well, her girlfriend and her, they were sitting across from me holding hands and she told me. Something like, "Mom, I've been a lesbian for a long time now and I just wanted it out in the open." I was more astonished by the way she told me. I mean sitting there holding hands with this girl. Blunt. More the way she told me than what she actually said. And then she went right into this little speech how she hoped that it was okay with me and that I had probably guessed anyways, but she didn't want to hear anything negative and if I had anything negative to say, well, she was just out of there. And that was it. She and her girlfriend stayed maybe a couple of more days, but they weren't around that much. Mostly they went out, I guess to the Village and the bars. We never talked about it after that.

Then she left to go back to San Francisco. I cried for days. But not about her being a lesbian. I cried because we had no real relationship. Because our relationship was awful. I cried because I wasn't the mother she wanted. I didn't blame myself that she was a lesbian although I did wonder if it had anything to do with getting love from a woman that she hadn't gotten from me. You see, I regret the kind of mother I was. I wasn't the greatest mother. And she's probably not the daughter I would have liked either.

She was hard to handle right from the beginning. Maybe colic. Whiny. Who knows? Her brother was three when she was born and he was kind of hyperactive. Or rather normally active for a boy. I don't know. I was trying to finish my degree and my husband wasn't around much. When he was, he really didn't want to be bothered so it was pretty much me and a lot of sitters. Our marriage wasn't that great either and I was depressed a lot of the time. Not the best thing for kids. A mother's tale of woe. Right? Not the kind of family life I had pictured. No question, we were dysfunctional.

Anyways, my husband left when she was about five. It was pretty mutual. I was tired of him and his outbursts and his control issues and, of course, there was a girlfriend waiting in the wings. It took me a few more years before I got my degree and a full time faculty position so there wasn't much money at the beginning. My husband had a good lawyer and the judge didn't award me much in terms of child support or alimony. Actually, it was better being a single parent in a lot of ways and Marci and her brother seemed okay. At least, at first. I never abandoned them. I always took care of them. I was never abusive although I was impatient and had kind of a bad temper back then. I was just busy struggling with being a single mom and finishing my thesis and having something of my own life. And it was exciting to be in New York with Women's Liberation just starting and I guess I wasn't around much. Certainly not emotionally. I did date a little. Men, not women, but nothing much came of it back then. I do have a boyfriend now.

I have to say I'm kind of self-centered and maybe back then, I didn't have that much capacity to love children the way that they needed. Self-preoccupied. I mean I loved them, but it was hard. I didn't enjoy them much those years when they were young. Who knew anything about bringing up kids back then. I guess I just didn't have that much empathy. Disconnected. I just felt like I was being swallowed up. By the time they were teenagers, they both had problems and both of them were in therapy. I had no control over Marci. We fought over everything. She disobeyed me constantly. We were screaming at each other all the time. Rules meant nothing to her. Took my things without asking. Her friends would come over when I wasn't home even though she knew they weren't supposed to. Refused to pitch in with chores and housework even though I was working full time. I knew she was doing drugs, but nothing terrible. Mostly pot. Experimental. Recreational, I think. It could have been worse. I worried most about her. Of course, her being a girl. But it wasn't all terrible, thank goodness. I have good memories too. I liked having older kids more than I did younger ones. Maybe a mother isn't supposed to say that, but I did. I took them lots of places. Theater. Concerts. New York is a great playground. We travelled. We had good times, I thought. Something Marci doesn't seem to remember.

Their father began to see them more once they were older. The idealized not-there father. That's the ironic thing. All charm and lots of money and it's hard for me to compete with his expensive gifts and expensive life style. I can't believe he's now the preferred parent when he was really this bastard. Do I sound bitter? I know I'm bitter. It seems so unfair. But I never said a bad word about him to them. He was their father and they had enough problems without me putting him down and affecting their relationship. That's one thing I do like about myself. Oh yes, I think he's okay about her being gay.

I wanted a daughter to be close to. To talk to, confide in. Like the same things. Do things together. Have similar interests. Different than my relationship with my own mother who was kind of distant and there wasn't much in common. I don't mean enmeshment. I do have my own life. But I have this girl who is rude and angry and critical, and won't miss a chance to put me down. My therapist—I'm always in therapy—says that Marci has this toxic effect on me. But I can't bring myself to stop seeing her. I just can't do that. But I'm just no match for her anger. Her outbursts. I withdraw and clam up, or say all the wrong things. Mostly I feel I annoy her. That I disappoint her. My friends tell me she'll outgrow it. That it's kind of an adolescent separation thing, an identity thing that's gone on too long. Maybe it's all the guilt I feel that makes me put up with it. Hang in. Try to make amends. The irony of it. Like that old Harry Chapin song about not being there for your kids when they're young. Then wanting to be close when they're older. Except then, they're not that interested. A kind of justice. Yes?

I am a better mother now for what it's worth. Marci and her girlfriend—a new one—just moved back east and are living in Brooklyn. I helped them out a lot until they both got jobs. I would bring over food, household stuff. Like that. I try to let them know that they can turn to me if they need anything. But there's just this estrangement. This distance. I tried to bring it up, but she doesn't want to talk about it. I've suggested we go to therapy together, but she says she doesn't have time. It's okay if I listen to her every word and agree with everything she has to say. She has no interest in me. Never a question about my work or my life. No interest that I joined PFLAG. She has all these negative opinions on what I'm like as a person. Like some fixed picture that won't change. I won't say she's wrong, but she just ignores the good stuff. But the confusing thing is, she calls me now. Stops over once in a while. It's like a mix of stay away, come back. I let her set the tone. I mean, if she wants to get closer on rare occasions, I get closer. If she wants to back off, I let her. I back off. Maybe it's too late. Maybe you can never make up for what you did or didn't do when they were young. It's a strange bond.

I worry about her. She has this awful temper and a lot of things set her off. She seems so out of control at times. She and her partner fight a lot and I know that it's sometimes physical. The neighborhood they live in is not that great either. So I worry about that too. And the bars they go to. She's not all bad. She's funny. She's smart. Generous too. She's got herself into graduate school and is doing well. So maybe she got some good stuff from me after all. I don't tell many people that she's a lesbian. I feel self-conscious. My good friends know. Some family. Maybe I think people will judge me as a mother. But it can't be anymore than I judge myself. My regrets, I think, are honest. I think I should have regrets.

My own parents were pretty strict. Very critical, judgmental. Especially my mother. Intrusive. Controlling. Trying to get you to feel guilty whenever she was displeased. Like whatever you did, you did to her. I brought up my own kids in a different time. I know I was too lenient. Letting them go their own way. Doing their own thing. Maybe before they were ready. I know I gave them too much independence. Maybe it was because of my own mother being so controlling. Probably it was because I wanted my own freedom.

I'd like to forgive myself. I tell myself that I did the best I could. That it can't be all me. There are genetics and my ex-husband was certainly part of it too. I do want her happy. I want her okay. I'd like to see her in a good relationship. My son is actually okay. Just got engaged. So maybe I will be a grandmother after all. But I see my children's emotional problems right up front. Their insecurities and I know, my ex-husband and I, we didn't give them the best start. But I can't undo what was done. I can only be the best mother and person that I can to my kids who are now grown up. I hope that means something to them. That's all I can really do. I'd really like us to be more of a family.

Lila, age fifty-six, was divorced, and lived in New York City. She was a professor and Dean of Students at a city university. Lila identified herself as Jewish, but called herself a secular atheist. She had two children. Her daughter Marci disclosed that she was a lesbian at age twenty-three in 1988. Lila said she was a feminist and was active in progressive and social justice movements including abortion rights, ERA, civil rights and the environment. She occasionally attended PFLAG meetings. Lila was interviewed in 1990.

14

Fran

SHE TOOK ME ON A RIDE I WASN'T PREPARED FOR

SHE, MY DAUGHTER ALICIA, said she wanted to tell us something. Fearing the worst, my husband thought that she was going to tell us she was HIV positive. I thought she was pregnant and that it was too late for an abortion. But she was smiling and happy. She said, "I came out." Just like that. We were stunned. Just stunned. It didn't make sense. She was always very popular. She always had boyfriends. Even when she went to college, a girl's college, and certainly there were plenty of opportunities there to come out, to be an active lesbian. But she didn't.

After college she lived with a boyfriend. Then she tells us that she came out. It seems that she put herself into therapy about a year and a half ago. We had no real knowledge of it although she did let it slip. But she never told us much and we didn't ask. What emerged was that she really was not interested in men. She was interested in women. I was just in a state of shock watching everything that developed after that. Actually, at the time that she came out, she was going out with a guy. I thought something happened to her. That was my feeling. That something went wrong. I didn't understand where it came from. But I also felt very helpless. I felt this was really beyond any resource that I had to change it. It wasn't that I didn't know gay people. But they weren't my daughter. They were friends. This is a different time in my life. I'm married now. I have a family.

It seemed like such an intellectual decision. She really didn't have any experience with women. It wasn't based on her meeting somebody and finding this was the right person to be with. It just seemed like it was all so academic. After that, she started to get active in the gay and lesbian community. She's so pretty and she had no trouble attracting young women. None whatsoever. But I was really concerned about her future and this path that she chose. I just thought her future would be more assured if she married some nice young guy who was on a nice career track. Now that was not going to be a possibility.

I tried to adjust to all of this. I thought that if she finds a partner, somebody who is more or less like herself, I could live with that. They would just be two attractive young women out in the world together and nobody was going to point fingers and say, "Oh my God, there's a lesbian couple!" So I was trying to come to terms with how things would be for her and for us and then it was kind of amazing because she got lots of phone calls. She was living with us then and these young women wanted to date her. It was a whole new world. The courtship process was amazing. These women made reservations at restaurants, got theater tickets, and bought her flowers. I never saw anything quite like this with any of her boyfriends and I didn't have much of that when I was dating.

All along she would keep us informed every single step of the way about everything that was happening to her. All I could say was, "Uh huh. Uh huh." I didn't know what to say. This is my daughter. I love her. I don't want to lose her. But I'm bewildered. I don't know what's going on. We were never controlling parents. We believed in letting our children find their own way. We weren't going to say, "No, no, no. You can't do this." That wouldn't work anyway. It was a new world. But it was kind of funny too.

She was dating a number of young ladies and then she's getting much more selective in people she's going out with. Then, being who she is, she comes out to the world which made me really nervous. She's a very forthcoming and outspoken person. She's not private or secretive and a lot of stuff would come out of her. If you asked questions, she would just tell you. Even if you didn't ask, she would tell you almost anything. She was firm about being out and it was something I really had to deal with. I was worried about her job for one thing. I mean there are certain areas of work where it's fine to be gay—but other areas of work, no.

I said to her, "What do you want to tell people at work for? You know people have lost their jobs over this issue." She said, "I want to tell people who I am." So she tells people that she works with and her best friend, of course, and a lot of people in our town that she was friendly with knew. Around that point, my husband and I decided we had a choice. We could either come out ourselves to our friends and families, or we can go in the closet and not tell anybody. As difficult as it was, we made the choice to come out to family members and close friends, even if they weren't so close. It was very difficult. Like holding your nose and jumping in. But most people were amazingly support-ive. There were people who were very surprised, but they were very supportive. Then there was this whole issue of her wanting to come out to her grandmother. That made me very nervous. I said, "Why do you need to do this? She could die at any time." She said, "It would be terrible if she died and she didn't know who I was." I had no control. This is what she wanted to do. She did whatever she wanted to do.

She was concerned about my emotional reactions and urged me to go to PFLAG. So I went to PFLAG. It was kind of interesting, but I was sort of detached. I knew people were listening to me but I didn't feel like anybody was really contributing a hell of a lot towards what I was going through. But I continued to go. I was so upset. I was so angry. I was so bewildered. How do you go from having a boyfriend to walking into the lesbian world? But it was not a phase that she was going through. She was embark-ing on territory where I couldn't follow. I couldn't pull her back. This was a significant turn in her life. I really felt that this was a major step in another direction and she seemed to have a lot of conviction about it.

But the biggest surprise of all came when she called up one day. She had moved into her own apartment. It was not okay for her to continue to live here. She didn't want to and I was quite worn out also by her being back home. She could have stayed as long as she wanted, but it was very exhausting. So then she calls to say that she decided that she wanted to find a butch partner. I say, "Okay." What am I supposed to say? Again, it felt to me like she's making all of these intellectual decisions. She never had any experience with a butch partner. She had never had any experience with any women until she came out and started dating a few young women.

So the next thing is that she called up some time later and she said she met someone. She said, "Mom, this relationship is really moving along very rapidly and I'd really like you to meet her." Okay. So they invite us to dinner and she is obviously very bright and shiny. She's very happy and I can't believe it. I was just stunned. Totally stunned. I mean her girlfriend looked like a guy. She's built like a guy. She wears men's clothes. I had to use the bathroom and I literally couldn't get myself to come out. It was getting awkward to be in the bathroom for that long but I just couldn't go out. Finally I pushed myself out. We made small talk. I was totally stunned.

She met her at one of the butch-femme groups when she decided she wanted a butch partner. In New York City, you can get anything you want. Right? There's a group for everything. So she went to a butch-femme group and that's where she first saw Caroline. She thought she was wonderful. She's very bright and she's very sharp and she's very funny. We get along very well. We kid each other back and forth a lot. But do I understand the choice? No. It's like she took me on a ride I wasn't prepared for and it got bumpier when she chose Caroline. I mean how it looks in the world. It's hard to understand the whole butch-femme thing, but this was a very deliberate choice on her part. She really was struck with Caroline and after knowing each other two weeks, she moved in with her and they've been together ever since. They're very committed. In fact, they just had a civil union ceremony in Vermont.

Caroline made it very clear to me when I met her. She said, "You know, I may look like this. I was born this way. But I'm a woman inside." Which was very hard for me to understand. I thought, "You do. You look like a guy." PFLAG parents talk about all the variations in this world and there are some parents—well, I could never could deal with their situations. One couple said their daughter moved back into their house with her partner who shaves. She's a woman, but she has all these male characteristics and she shaves like a man shaves. Everyday. I guess transgender.

So that would be harder for me than Caroline. Much harder. But Caroline told me, "I'm going to marry your daughter. You'll see." I thought, "Oh my God!" I had to go to the bathroom again. It was very hard for me to go public with Caroline. We have family events and whatever went on, they were always included. It was very hard. Do I tell my daughter this? No. I don't tell her because it's my struggle. She might listen, but she's not going to change anything. You understand. All worry. No power. You have no power as parents. I could ride along, or not and lose her. I was totally overwhelmed.

I felt like she was pulling away and I was very upset because I thought Caroline was going to move her out to the woods someplace and I wouldn't know what's going on. I had very little private time with her. It was always with Caroline. My husband told me to call her up and say I would like to have some private time with her. So I did. She came over and I told her how I felt and that life had changed so much and she was going to be totally taken over by Caroline and taken away from her family. We talked and talked until about three in the morning. I told her that I wondered what did I have to do with it. She told me about her boyfriends, what her experiences were with each one, how unsatisfactory they really were, and how satisfactory it is for her to be with Caroline. She talked all about how she felt growing up and one of the things that came out was that she said that being a lesbian had nothing to do with either of us. That we didn't cause this. She said, "I think it's just genetics."

She has a very, very good relationship with Caroline who has really been terrific in her life. They are extraordinarily happy and I think it's been very positive that she's really happy and committed in this relationship. I think it's tough in our society to be doing this. Actually, the interesting thing is that after she came out, we got to be much, much closer. So that is a very nice by-product. Really, this whole thing has been just a process of continually adjusting to what's happening next.

Fran, age seventy-two, was college educated and had worked as a fashion designer before marrying. She had three children. Her daughter Alicia disclosed that she was beginning to identify as a lesbian at age twenty-six in 1995, and she and her partner, Caroline were joined in civil union in Vermont in 2000. Fran was a member of PFLAG *and supportive of progressive and social justice causes. She lived in Westchester County, New York and was interviewed in 2000.*

15

Naomi

PARENTS DO LEAVE KIDS ON HILLSIDES

WELL, INITIALLY, SHE TOLD ME she thought she was bisexual. I wasn't shocked at all. It was really okay with me. I didn't need to get involved in PFLAG or anything because I didn't feel like I needed a support group. I have friends who are gay. One of my closest friends has a gay daughter. We have lesbian-couple friends and the community I live in is a very liberal, progressive community. New York, you know. I don't have any piece of my life that gives me a problem with it. But I had a hard time with the bisexual part. I wanted her to make up her mind. It was making me nuts. Half of me was saying that she was going to be involved with men and maybe get married and have babies. The other half was saying maybe that wouldn't happen. The idea of being bisexual for me was like a constant back and forth, which I found very unnerving.

Actually, I felt kind of stupid. She played with trucks. She played with boys. She never played with dolls. Cabbage Patch for a short time after I gave in to her adopting a doll which I thought was disgusting. But she didn't really play with it. She just wanted it. She got into a lot of confrontations for all kinds of reasons and was a child who was always in jeans because she'd rip a dress to pieces when she was crawling. She was always doing something physical. Why would you put a kid like that in a dress especially since I'm always in jeans? But I never thought there was anything wrong. When we had to go somewhere and I wanted to put her in something that was more feminine, like a dress, she would do it.

She was five and a half months when we adopted her. I have a picture of her in a tiny crib in the baby home in China and that's what she lived in for five months. The only exercise I think the babies got was to get them on the floor occasionally and roll them around. But who we adopted was this incredibly active, incredibly athletic and bright child. Not a book person, not a reader, and with a slight learning disability, but who just flourished when she was active. With a biological child you can have certain assumptions about who they will look like. What they'll be good at. I always felt that with an adopted child, my job was to keep all the doors open so she could figure out what she wanted to do. Because we didn't know what her family did or what their strengths were. And we never knew what she'd look like as an adult. I used to look at Asian people on the street when she was an infant because I had no idea what she'd look like as a grown up. I did think that what might be difficult for her was a Jewish environment which is very heavy on education. Most of our friend's children are students and do very well in school. Janie is not interested. It's not who she is.

It wasn't difficult to tell people. It was easy. Most of the people I told were not surprised. But some were. Somebody said, "She can't be. She's gorgeous." But I've been very independent thinking all my life and I don't really let other people's values bother me too much. I stick to what I feel is right. But even though, I still think a lot about what other people think of me. What I did. What I might have contributed. Has to be the mother. It's wrong, but the way it is with boys that are gay is because of their mothers. They had a weird relationship with their mother. Right? No. With lesbian women, I don't know.

Janie had dated some boys, but it was more that she had friendships with these guys. None of that female insanity that I remember from being a teenager and worrying about if a guy was going to call. She never really went through that. So she didn't have that hormonal craziness that goes on at that stage. Janie's very attractive and boys and men were always attracted to her. But it made her kind of angry. I just thought that she had trouble having relationships with people. She was so tough on people and I think felt a little scared to really commit and get involved because of loss. Because of the adoption and all the other stuff that happened, or didn't happen in the orphanage. It did upset me because I didn't want her to go through life not having wonderful, healthy, passionate relationships. For me, that's always been the most important thing in my life. So when she came out, I thought maybe now she'll be able to have those feelings. Because she didn't have it with the boys she dated.

I will say there was a very funny moment when she had a lot of clothes here and I needed something from her closet. A friend of mine was here and we opened the closet door and she looked at the closet and she said it looked like her son's closet. What had happened was that slowly the clothes that she had which were much more feminine disappeared and the closet was filled with more masculine stuff. The biggest moment was for Janie to tell her grandmother who was in her eighties and constantly, constantly bombarding me with, "Is she seeing anyone? Is she in love with anyone?" My mother was very intrusive. You could never tell her it's none of your business. My mother grew up in a very Victorian environment where the biggest concern was what other people would say. I felt all along that Janie needed to do it because my mother was old and not in great shape at that point. She died a year later. We had long talks about how to do it and Janie did tell her. I was very proud of my daughter and very proud of my mother for accepting it. The rest of the family doesn't. They're Orthodox Jews. But they still adore Janie. My mother's death brought everybody up here and Janie had a girlfriend that she had just gotten involved with right around the time my mother was dying. We had everybody at dinner and she had this girl come. I had already called to let my cousins know and Janie was really concerned about how they would feel because she does know about their attitudes about homosexuality. But it's been fine.

She's been in two significant relationships and the most recent one for a year. I haven't especially liked either of them and she knows that. They're welcome here and I do make the effort. But they've both been stormy relationships. I mean a lot of anger and physical hitting. She seems to be very attracted to Latina women, and that's the community she basically lives in. But I have great reservations and serious fears about these relationships. I don't believe that they're healthy. To be very honest, I think one of the reasons that she feels very comfortable in Latino culture is because there is a more diverse racial appearance. There's gradation in looks, in color. She gets very close to the parents of any close girlfriend she has. Like she always makes sure that she has a secondary family. She did that when she was in school. She developed very intense relationships with her friends' parents. I always say it's a backup system in case I disappear. She always has a backup system. But of all the girlfriends she's chosen, Janie is definitely the most intellectual one.

She went down to live in Texas a couple of years ago. I was terrified because she's out front about her racial identity, her Jewish identity, and her gay identity. She wears a rainbow thing around her neck with a Jewish star hanging from it. I was absolutely terrified as was everybody else. That she'd be in a place like where Matthew Shepherd lived. The first thing people see is that she's Asian and that's primary in a society that is racist. It overwhelms anything else. She's just more likely to get bashed around there being Asian before they even find out that she's gay or Jewish. Lately she told me she wants to live in New York again. Here I don't worry so much. She's a real street kid. She takes care of herself. She knows how to operate here. But she's aggressive and will take somebody on physically and so I worry about that. I'm talking about safety. But we're living in a time when this is all pretty out in the open and there are enough communities and places that people can find that are comfortable.

I think we're very close, but we haven't figured out how to be with each other. We've had very difficult times. I can have very high expectations of people and Janie has grown up pushing the envelope with me—and I give in. You can't take advantage of her. But she can take advantage of me. She's tough and I'm real easy. I was no match for her. My boyfriend used to get crazed at the way she spoke to me and I allowed a lot of behaviors that other people might not have allowed. In language and the way she spoke to me—and the way that she dealt with me throughout her life. That is, until very recently.

I would get scripts from friends before I spoke to her about certain things that I wanted to discuss. I would talk it out with friends and I actually wrote down what I was going to say so that I could stick to the script because she was so good at getting me off it. Then I would still end up being the one at fault. It goes back to, well, all tied up with being a good mother and being there for her no matter what. I wanted her to know that no matter what, I'm her mother and I was going to be there for her. I think that she's taken advantage of that and I've allowed it. That's what we go through. But there's another piece to it.

There was in our synagogue—a Rosh Hashanah children's service one time that was something about Abraham and Isaac and the fact that Abraham doesn't go through with sacrificing Isaac. The lesson was supposed to be that parents never leave their children alone on a hillside. Or something like that. I had a friend with me who also had an adopted child, a son, and we looked at each other and started crying. We both know that's bullshit. It's very different from biological children. Parents do leave kids on hillsides and our kids know the truth. That's the one truth that our kids know. They know that it can happen because it's happened to them. And the job of an adoptive mother is to make up for that and it's very difficult.

Janie woke up one night when her father had to go to the hospital. She was about four and he'd been ill before so she was very scared. He told her he'd be back from the hospital before she woke up in the morning and she went to bed absolutely terrified that he was really sick. She got really crazed. All of a sudden she walked in our bedroom and said, "Does she know my name?" And I said, "She? The sitter? Who? What woman are you talking about?" And she said, "You know, that woman in whose uterus I grew. Does she know my name?" I told her that she had a Chinese name and that it was on the papers that we got when we brought her over, and she wanted to look at them. So there's things she'll need to figure out.

When she was eighteen, her behavior was so bad that I threw her out because she was physical towards me. I had been away for three months and I had given her plenty of warning that this one girlfriend couldn't stay here anymore. When I came home, we had this huge thing and Janie kicked my door in. I always felt that if the door hadn't been there, she might have actually hit me. I threw her out and she hasn't lived here since. Throwing her out was major and the only time she's ever said to me something about being adopted. I told her that I loved her dearly, but she couldn't stay here because I was afraid to be with her and I couldn't live with anyone who I'm afraid to be with. It was important for me to do this. I know she knows that I'm here for her if there's an emergency and there did come a point when she finally realized that I'll always be here for her. So I've stopped letting her beat me up.

What I liked about myself as a mother was my being there. Fulfilling what I said I would do for Janie, no matter what. And recently she seems to get it. That I really am there even though I kicked her out of the house. Even though I don't let her take advantage of me. We talk, but now we don't see each other very much. But I'm there. Even when I'm out of the country, she always can get me. She knows that. And that, I think, is what I gave. We are slowly rebuilding our relationship and it's taking time. But I think a lot of it is her age and breaking away.

Her being a lesbian is not the issue. I think there was a period in the beginning where I was uncomfortable and she was very uncomfortable also, like getting undressed in front of each other. We used to run around here naked all the time. I'm always running around naked or half-naked. I had weird feelings because it suddenly changed. The whole sexual aspects of this thing. I wouldn't get undressed in front of my son. How does that work if your child is a lesbian? The one thing I miss very much is that I can't tell jokes to my daughter about male-female sexual relationships. I miss having those kinds of funny things that women share about men. And I miss shopping with her. Although when she comes in, we shop together but we really don't shop together. She's always in one section of the Gap and I'm in the other. We're not together.

These are things that came up for me. She had a girlfriend sleep over and I said to her that she needed to let me know what kind of girlfriend this is. Because if this is a sexual relationship, she's got to sleep in the living room. If it were a guy that she was having a relationship with, he'd be sleeping in the living room. It just would have been more obvious if it had been a male. She looked at me and I said, "I'm serious. If you're gay, why do rules not apply that would apply if you were heterosexual? I'm not ready to have you sleep in the same bed with your sex partner in my home. I don't care what they look like or where they are from. I'm not ready, so you got to be honest with me."

She did ask me to go to movies with her. Lesbian movies. I told her I had no interest in going. I don't know how she took that. I don't like to go to particularly graphic movies of any kind and if there's any sort of graphic sex in it, it doesn't interest me. Heterosexual or homosexual. I do watch a program that deals with a lot of gay issues. I don't have a problem with that. But I wouldn't go with my daughter to a movie that was X-rated heterosexually. I've said to her that I'd love to go to one of the clubs she goes to. She's a real clubber. It's her thing and I love to dance. She said the music is too loud and I probably wouldn't enjoy it. But I've said we could go early or something. I really would like to go.

I'm very happy that we have couples that are gay and lesbian that she knows around here on a normal basis and that she talks with them. We've gone to Gay Reform synagogue services. I'd like her to meet a nice Jewish girl, but she's not interested in Jewish lesbians. But at least she's in a Jewish environment sometimes. One of the biggest things for me was if she was going to marry a Jew. It didn't matter to me so much when she was younger, but it always sort of did a little. She's grown up in a Jewish community and the value systems and the piece of her that's Jewish, well I don't want her to lose that. I see her as Jewish. Maybe if she got involved in Asian culture, she's not going to be Jewish. But both pieces of her are important. She hasn't tackled the Asian piece really and that's up to her. I've told her that we can go to China whenever she wants. She can go with me. Or without me. My cousin has a business in China and he suggested she go with him. Whether she'd be accepted there is a very big thing. She's really got a lot of stuff to deal with, but she's also at the age where what you do is figure out who you are.

I'd say I was the kind of mother who never missed a game and got such pleasure from watching this child play Little League. Regrets? Yeah. I think that I wasn't mothering enough. I never made dinner, if I could help it. I didn't play games with her very much. I hated going to playgrounds. Wouldn't do it if I didn't have to. All that stuff. I just didn't like talking about Pampers or whatever.

So I feel that I didn't mother her in that respect. Her father and I ended up getting divorced and I remarried for a very short time, but it was wrong and I ended it. So there's been a lot of changes in our lives. I've had depression at different times too and I think that was terrible for her to live through. I think that there was so much going on with me that I wasn't mothering enough even though I was here physically. It's not that I was selfish, but there was a lot going on and she could have used a more stable home life. It's a regret, but it's nothing I can do anything about.

The one place where Janie had problems was when her father and I separated. He was involved with someone who was very jealous of their relationship and incredibly jealous of me. I couldn't call the house because it got her upset. But my greatest thing was keeping Janie's father involved so that they could develop what they have now. Now they don't need me to be involved at all. But I had to remind him back then to call her, to spend time with her, and to be included in every discussion that we've had that had to do with parenting issues. The result is that they have an incredibly wonderful relationship, second to me, and that probably is one of the things I'm most proud of because that was very difficult to do. She doesn't know how often when he did call her, it was because I had called him a minute before and said, "Call your daughter."

I want her to have children. I can't see her not having children because she has such incredible joy from them. But I could never see her being pregnant because it just never seemed to go with this kind of active person. When she came out as bisexual, I thought maybe there'd be a man around so she'd have a biological child. But she could adopt which was always a part of our life and always a possibility. It's not that I want grandchildren, but it's because children are so important to her. She's so wonderful with them. I think she would be an incredible parent. Because underneath this exterior of "I'm in charge, I'll take care of myself, and I'll hold my own bottle" that she had as an infant, there's this mushy interior that's full of all this tenderness that just pours out of her whenever she's around a child. It's palpable. She's like the Pied Piper. They follow her everywhere.

I have concerns about what would happen if she did have a biological child with another woman because her relationships have been so unstable and she isn't really settled. So my concern is that if she got involved with somebody and did have a baby. I mean the legal aspects of her having a child that someone else carries which isn't hers and how that would work if they're not in a committed relationship. And my attaching to a child and then having that child not be my grandchild in any way is a very upsetting thought. So I think about how I can help her do it in a way that will protect her right to that child. That's my real concern.

I do think that I'm more comfortable with sex between two women than two men. My friends and I are always running around asking one of our very closest lesbian friends if there is a course they can give us on how to be a lesbian. Because these men are such a pain in the ass and they're all going to die off early anyways and we'll be left together. Please. I'm only joking.

Naomi, age fifty-six, was divorced and employed as a social worker. She identified herself as Jewish. Her one child, Janie, was adopted and of Chinese origin. She disclosed that she was a lesbian at age eighteen in 1996. Naomi lived in New York City and was active in the Disability Rights movement. She was interviewed in 2001.

16

Cheryl

HER LESBIANISM IS THIRD IN LINE

A S A CHILD, JODY WAS ALWAYS UNHAPPY. Something was not right. She was struggling with something. This was my only child. A much loved child. I was divorced when she was seven and she and I have always been very close. I thought her father and I handled the divorce as best we could. She maintained a relationship with him and his family and still does because I always thought it was important for a girl to have a relationship with her father. But she just couldn't be happy.

The day that Jody told me she was a lesbian was very emotional. There were a lot of tears when she told me, but I was not shocked. I did the best I could to let her know that it was okay with me and I just tried to be as supportive as possible. She told me while we were driving to visit Allie, this friend of hers who turned out to be her partner. Allie had been hospitalized for anorexia and it was terrible for my daughter and me to see how much she had disintegrated. Jody and Allie had been very close and she lived with us for a while. I did have some serious inklings. They shared a room and I always knocked on her door before going in there. But when I would open the door, they would be more than just asleep in the same bed. Hugging. Embracing. Now the thing that's happened that was so traumatic was when Allie got out of the hospital, she got a boyfriend. Maybe to make sure that she was heterosexual and not gay.

The cutting started when Jody was sixteen. She was cutting herself and really couldn't figure out why. I loved her no matter what and when I became aware that she was cutting, I just did what I always do. I bought books about it and read as much as I could. She couldn't explain it to me because she didn't understand. She just knew that she had no control and had to do this. When I look back now, I'd say she was probably struggling with coming out and didn't know how to deal with it. It was like she just couldn't figure out what was making her unhappy or why she didn't feel like other kids. I remember—this was just before she came out to me—she had her own room with a big wall with nothing on it, so she decided to put up all pictures of men. I think she was trying to be like everybody else. She didn't know anybody that was a lesbian. She did tell me later that some of her friends in high school knew that she was a lesbian before she did.

My daughter has been in therapy and on antidepressants since she was about sixteen and she began to do much better. She graduated high school and went on to college. She's a very, very bright girl, but she had to go to a college that's not up to her potential because her doctor wanted her to stay near home. When she went to college, she joined an organization of lesbian, gay, and straight students and became very active. She told me later that when she went to the orientation, the first thing she did was to find other gay students. They had booths at orientation, but there were not a lot of gays at her college.

But the other thing that happened was she had been doing a lot of drinking and drugs which I was not aware of. I always thought of myself as a mother who was very in touch with my child. I mean, we've been very close. We talked every day. We had a good relationship. But I was completely clueless. She said to me, "Mom, I think I have a serious alcohol and drug problem. I need to get into treatment." We always talked about what she did and she checked in with me. But never, never, ever did I detect that she was drinking. It's mind boggling to me that I missed the signs. Maybe she was that good a con artist.

So I'm thinking that all of this has to do with her struggles of not being able to fit in, and if you're at college and you want to fit in with a group, the thing to do is—well, everybody gets drunk. She told me her problem was that she couldn't stop and she couldn't function even though the other kids could. So she went into drug and alcohol treatment. I give her a lot of credit for doing that because she was nineteen years old. I just said to myself that I was glad it happened when she was nineteen instead of forty-nine. She was in an in-patient place for about three weeks, then in a group home and then outpatient. I would go visit her and met some of the people that were there and through all of this, she was always struggling because Allie wasn't around and had this boyfriend.

So anyway, come to find out that Jody and another patient were having sex. It turned out he was a drug addict from a poor area of the city, separated from his wife, and had a child. Not an appropriate person. I just assumed she just kind of did it to experience sex with a guy. I don't know why. Maybe he showed some kind of interest in her. Supportive, I guess. So anyway, she had sex with this man. Maybe she was wishing she wasn't a lesbian because that would make the break with Allie easier. But it didn't work for her and as she looks back at it now, it was a big huge mistake. She realizes it was bad judgment, a bad decision related to alcoholism. When she told me he was a drug user, we went and had her tested. I was so worried about AIDS, but she was negative. But through it all, she was able to focus on her schoolwork.

She lives at home now because she decided that the worst place for her to be was on campus because of the drinking. She's been sober for eight months and for a while was going to a meeting every day. Now she probably goes about three or four times a week. Meetings are very important to her. She also goes to a gay and lesbian youth center. She's always trying to see where she belongs. She does have a girlfriend and brings her home. I think she's a very nice girl. Jody met her through AA and she has a drug addiction. I don't think this is the best time to be in a relationship because they're both struggling with their addictions. But they seem to be first and foremost good friends and able to support each other. I think this isn't the love of her life, but they go to dances and do things together. I don't like them sleeping together in my house even though she promises they won't have sex. Her girlfriend did come over this one night and she was tired and instead of driving home, she stayed at our house and the two of them said, "Now don't worry. We're not going to have sex." I said, "This is like way more information than I want." I told her that if this was a boy, he wouldn't be sleeping over. I wouldn't let her sleep with a boyfriend in her room.

My concerns are that I always wanted her to be safe. I don't want her to make a million dollars. I wanted her to be safe and I wanted her to be happy. What bothers me is the world. Society. How she is judged. I think about this awful situation where this boy was tied to a fence and beaten. I think of the jokes that you just hear out in the world or on television. Little hurtful comments. My whole life I've just been so worried about her being unhappy. I guess when you hear these offhanded remarks about gays, I assume that if you're a lesbian, you're able to deal with it. Like any other minority. I suppose being her mother, it's harder for me than for her. I'm annoyed at the Catholic Church's stand. Not that I'm considering leaving the church, but I am considering finding a different church to go to. Because I believe they, including the Pope, have got it wrong.

I have one friend who I've confided in and, of course, my immediate family. But I've not told my extended family, or other friends or people that I work with. I guess I hoped it was a stage that she was going through. She's come out to her friends, to my immediate family, and to her father. But my ex-husband's somebody who is almost not there. He's emotionally not there for her. What also happened is that Jody is overweight and right now, she's probably the heaviest she's ever been. She's cut off all her hair and her father's comment was, "You look like a lesbian." It was like that it was bad enough to be a lesbian, but do you have to look like a lesbian? And she also has a problem with him regarding her alcoholism because he's not at all supportive of what she's doing to help herself. He does not believe in going to meetings. He does not believe in therapists. The first thing he said to her when she told him she was an alcoholic was not to blame him because he drank. So it's always all about him. I think he called her a dyke. And whatever that word means, I guess it's tough to hear it said to your face.

My daughter told my mother and she kind of regrets it. My mother is seventy-four years old and was a widow since she was thirty-nine. She raised her children by herself, doesn't drive, and kind of lives in a little bubble. Jody told her in a kind of flip way and I know she regrets that she wasn't more gentle. But my mother doesn't really understand it at all and told me she really would rather Jody hadn't told her. My mother doesn't understand the alcohol. She would never understand the cutting so I never got her involved in that because I knew she couldn't handle that either. When I was trying to comfort my own mother about my daughter's lesbianism, I told her it was really not a choice for Jody. If you were going to choose a life, you wouldn't choose a gay or lesbian life so young. My mother lost my father very early. He died when I was sixteen. She had four children and the youngest was nine. My mother's Irish-Catholic. She's just kind of like, you just keep moving forward. Just put food on the table. So the four of us really kind of raised ourselves. My mother kept a roof over our heads, but she never let us talk about our father dying. Only as adults did we ever get to talk about it. I missed a lot as a child. I wanted to know my child. My mother didn't know me.

I didn't want Jody to suffer. It's going to be tough for her as a lesbian. That's just my preconceived notion. I guess what I have to realize is I cannot make Jody's life easier. Like the other day, we had a big family wedding. Jody had just recently shaved her head and bleached it. She's always had beautiful hair. She tells me that it's her hair, and she's right. I have no control over what she's going to look like. I have a picture of my daughter on my desk that was taken at one of her birthday parties. She was very low in her weight. She had beautiful hair and she's a pretty girl. I said, "Look at how beautiful your hair was." And she goes, "Mom, I was so miserable at that point in my life." So she was a beautiful young teenager and was cutting herself and drinking and doing drugs because she was so unhappy. So how important is hair and what you look like.

I think the one philosophy I've always had is that I gave my daughter credit for having a brain in her head. It's kind of like how I deal with the world. I never want to insult anybody's intelligence. So with her, this was probably a mistake because maybe I overestimated her. I mean she still was a kid. I just was the mother who encouraged her to go out, have fun, do whatever you're going to do—and I was always on the couch waiting. I really did not have a social life. Never dated. My life was pretty wrapped up in her since I got divorced. So she really never saw me in a relationship. When I think of being married and how I used to feel, I remember driving up to the house and seeing my ex-husband's car and I'd get this upset feeling that I don't have anymore. So for me, it was better being divorced. I've been in therapy, but I guess I kind of put me on the back burner, making sure Jody was getting what she needed. I think she's having trouble leaving me. But she's got to. She's got to. We rely on each other too much.

I think we probably are as close as we have always been, but I don't know enough about lesbianism so I don't know her hopes and dreams. Where she'll be able to live and feel comfortable. Is it so important that you know a person is gay? If you're coming out, do you want people to know that you're gay so you do it by your appearance? How you look? Especially with kids, it's like, "This is who I am. I'm going to show the world who I am." Flaunt it, I guess. If you're coming out, you want people to know that you're gay.

I have a friend who told me she had struggled through two marriages and is now in a third. She said, "You know, I wish I was a lesbian because being married is a tough life." I believe that I'm heterosexual, but I have not been involved with a man since my divorce so it's almost like I'm asexual. I do hope my daughter finds a sex life that she can enjoy. But she's been in two relationships and both of them have been so troubled. One was an anorexic that nearly died and this girl that she's with right now was sexually abused by her brother for ten years—and verbally and physically abused by her father. She uses alcohol and cocaine and her mother threw her out of the house. She has terrible, terrible dreams. I just think that life shouldn't be this hard. I've learned that a lot of parents try to change their children or were not at all supportive or completely disown their children. I could not do any of those things. First and foremost, I love my daughter.

I don't think you hold a baby in your arms and say that you hope she's going to be a lesbian. I probably will not have any grandchildren. I'm interested in going to a PFLAG meeting because I want to hear how other people deal with it. My daughter would like me to join PFLAG and I did join Families Anonymous. It's kind of like Al-Anon for parents. But it can't consume my life. I've been a little afraid of PFLAG because I haven't really been able to come out and I don't know whether they would force you to before you're ready. But I'm probably no good to her unless I can deal with it. As my daughter said, I guess I just better get with the program. Those have been my struggles, but I'm struggling most with her psychological well being. Her cutting was very serious. Her alcohol and drug addictions are very serious. Actually, her lesbianism is third in line. It's almost like a piece of cake.

Cheryl, age fifty, was divorced and worked for an insurance company. She identified herself as Catholic. Her one child, Jody ,disclosed that she was a lesbian when she was eighteen in 1998. Cheryl had yet to join PFLAG, but was beginning to think about attending meetings. She lived in Connecticut and was interviewed in 2000.

CONNECTION

17
Shirley

GOD, WATCH OVER HER FOR ME, EVERYDAY

I KNEW SHE WAS GAY. But I was afraid to say anything to her. I was afraid I might put something in her head. But I'd been watching Annie. She's not pregnant. Annie is a lesbian. Annie's gay. One night I didn't know where she was. I'm praying. "God help me that Annie call me." Walking back and forth, back and forth and I'm going crazy. I said, "God, I'm sending this message to Annie. Please let Annie call me." In about a half an hour the phone rings.

I said, "Hi honey. Where are you?" She said, "I'm with my friend." I said, "Don't lie to me, Annie." And she said, "Mommy, I'm coming home in a second." When she got home, I saw in her face that she was sad. Annie was depressed because she in her mind was thinking what's gonna happen to me today with my mother. She said, "Mommy, sit down." And she sits very close to me. She said, "Mommy, I'm a lesbian." Don't tell me it didn't hurt me. It hurt me. It hurt me way inside. Make me cry for days. For days I cried, but I never let her know that I'm crying. Never. I always cried at night, very secretly. I would go to the bathroom. But I am positive Annie knew I was crying because you could have seen it in my face even though I would wash my face. I would cry on the train. Cry at my job. Things like that, you know.

Then both of us sit down and had a very long talk. I can't remember the talk so good, but I hug her up and I say, "Annie, I love you. Annie, I will always love you." And we keep hugging each other really tight. She told me that she would go to the Village every afternoon. I guess she was inquiring about different things. Then she said, "Mommy, you want to go with me to a gay meeting?" I said, "Yes, I'm very happy to go to see what's going on." I'm her mother, you know and I would like to know what's going on in the community. We went to a PFLAG meeting maybe less than a week after she told me. She took me there and I saw all these people. Mothers and daughters. Getting all together to say my daughter's a lesbian or my son is gay. I went and I surprised myself. When my turn comes, I said, "My daughter is Annie. I am her mother. My daughter is a lesbian." And everybody clap and all these women they came to me and they shake my hand. Some of them hug me and ask me how long my daughter told me that she's a lesbian. I said, "Just five days ago."

We still talked every day, but Annie was a little nervous, very tense where I'm concerned. I still felt so depressed. I wasn't eating like how I should. I wasn't talking to anybody. I didn't have friends to talk to. I call my sister and I told her. And she says, "That's your daughter, you know. You have to love her. I don't care what she tells you. That's your daughter." I said, "I know. I will always love Annie." Then after I started going to the meetings, I started going down to the Village. I started going to the parade. I started to look at different things like what's going on in the gay community. If I see something, I say, "Annie, who is this? A girl or a boy?" I did all this because I love Annie so much that I think I have to live in her world. I have to know every little thing that's going on there. Everything. That's what pushes me.

Of course, I used to feel bad for her. Sad for her. Won't have my grandchildren. Wouldn't see Annie married. A lot of things was going through my mind. I always thought that she would get married. I thought I will take care of Annie's children, my grandchildren. I would go to Annie's house and stay there and do things for Annie. Like all mothers will do for her children and her grandchildren. And then, so one day I sit down and I talk to myself. Annie could still have children. But she would never get married. Things like that and I started to laugh real loud. I said to myself, "What the hell you crying for? You crying like Annie died. What's the matter with you? Annie's still alive and I should be proud to have this daughter. I brought her into this world.

Pull your life together and be happy. Let Annie see you happy. Be yourself. Like how you used to be."

Then I started to ask questions. I said, "Annie, how long you knew you felt like this?" Because I wasn't depressed anymore so I could talk to Annie freely. Annie told me, "Mommy, remember this girl who used to come home and play with me?" And Annie told me she had loved that girl. I'm talking about a young kid. Maybe like five or six years old. And she was getting the feeling that she loved this girl, but she didn't know how to. How do I put it? She didn't know why these feelings was coming to her, but she loved this other girl. And I said, "Oh my God, from so young!" She said, "Yes." I said, "But you used to love boys." She said, "I liked them, but not the same way. I wouldn't marry them or anything." Different things we would talk about. I asked her questions and she would tell me. Once she said "Mommy, you know. I could still have children if I want to."

But I don't feel like I used to feel. I'm free inside. I feel much better inside. I even tell a friend that Annie is gay. I call up her one day when I'm watching a show about these children that are gay and some of the parents. How the parents treated the children so bad. And this mother on the show said, "I won't tell anybody you gay." Then I said to myself, "Oh, my gosh. I never tell anyone of my friends that Annie was gay. Maybe I'm ashamed of it." But no, I'm not ashamed of it. I talk to people all over and people know that Annie is gay. Why should I be ashamed? That's my daughter.

I told my girlfriend. I said, "Girl, I have something to tell you. Annie is a lesbian." And she said, "No, Annie can't be a lesbian." I said, "Don't insult Annie. Can't hear it, you know." But then she said, "No, I don't mean anything. I work with two gay men and I love these men a lot. I respect you and I respect your daughter." Then she said, "How do you feel about it? Now you tell me about it." I said, "Everything takes time." And then she said, "Well, how is the relationship between you and your daughter? It's still close?" I said, "I think myself and Annie became much closer than how we used to be. Now myself and Annie get very tight together. Very, very, very close. We talk about anything and everything." And she said, "Well, I'm very happy to hear that."

You see, I would like to tell other friends about my daughter, but then I don't want people to talk about my daughter. That's what I don't want. You wouldn't like to see me in the evening when you was alone because you know a mother could get very angry if somebody say something about her daughter or her son. She can get very, very, very angry with that person. And she can even hurt that person. This certain girl called me and she said, "Did you see that?" I said, What?" She said, "On TV. Gay people parade." I said, "Oh, I go to the Gay and Lesbian Parade." She said, "I know you would not go there." I said, "Please don't tell me where I cannot go. I choose where I want to go because these two legs belong to me alone." Every time you criticize the gay community, it really gets to me because I know my daughter is a lesbian. I don't want to hear people criticizing because it's my daughter they are criticizing.

PFLAG helped me. It helped me, but I don't go anymore. Because Annie doesn't go there anymore. Annie has her own life to live. But I would be very happy to go back if Annie wants to. Because it's nice to go there and express your feelings to these other parents. Even to the children. Because you go there and you hear different people talking. Different mothers. Different lesbian children. Different gay children. You hear them talking about their parents. Some children can't tell their parents. Other women talking about still trying to come into it. About their son or their daughter being gay or lesbian. And then I said to myself, "What the hell they talking about? It's their child. Why can't they tell their child that they love them? But don't tell a child you love them if you feel sorry for them. You have to love your child because that's your child. You have to go with an open mind. That's all I'm asking these mothers." Now me, I had to move on and I had to accept my daughter because she is mine. God knows in my heart how much I love that girl.

Sometimes, I'm going to work and I sit in the train. I'm Catholic and I'm always praying with my rosary beads. My eyes will get tears for the love I feel for Annie. And sometimes some things come in my mind and I say, "God, if anybody hurts Annie, what I'm gonna do?" I think what I'm gonna do to them if they hurt Annie. Sometimes I don't want Annie to come home late because

I'm scared somebody will hurt her. But Annie doesn't understand that. I'm scared Annie alone coming home because she's gay. Because there's a lot of people hate gay people. In the subway around here. You hear these young boys and they talking and you can see murder in these boy's eyes. And you want to have a fight with all of them. I'm thinking about Annie and I say, "God walk with her. God be with her. God watch over her for me, everyday." Annie don't know why I'm so worried about her. Somebody's with Annie, I'm not worried at all. But when you alone out to walk the streets, you don't know you might meet a gang. A hateful gang. And a lot of these gangs are the type that kill gay men. All these things I'm thinking about my daughter alone out there.

I would be very happy to go back to PFLAG. Even though most of the parents was White. I think we were the only Black people that was there. It doesn't bother me because I'm gonna tell you something. I deal with a lot of White people so why should it bother me if they're White or they're Black. I'm here to hear different parents' versions. How you talk about your child. And the ones that hate their children, somebody can put some sense into their head and talk to them and say, "Ma'am, that's your child. If you hate your child, don't you know other people gonna hate your child too. And if you love your child, other people look at you. What are they gonna say? I'll tell you. They're gonna say, 'Oh, my gosh! Look at this lady. Her daughter's a lesbian. But look how she loves her daughter.'"

When I went to the Gay Parade two years ago, I told Annie I should have a T-shirt. She said, "Mommy, you in a T-shirt?" I said, "Yes, Annie." We went to this guy and he printed a beautiful T-shirt for me. I don't remember what it said, but let me tell you I couldn't walk from here to the subway with that T-shirt on. But when I get to the city, I could wear my T-shirt. You wouldn't believe it. Even the postman was complimenting me. You should see my T-shirt. I have it in a special place. And this White woman came to me. More than one White woman came to me. No Black woman didn't come to me. Only White women alone. And they come to me with their daughters. You know what they told me? They ask me where did you get this T-shirt from? I said, "These are my own words." And everybody, even the Black girls, they're calling me Mommy. The White and the Black young women was calling me Mommy. Some of them said, "Oh I wish you was my mother. Could you be my mother for today?" And I said, "I'm everybody's mother." I became everybody's mother.

Well, this White lady especially came to me and she was a Jewish lady too. And this lady's daughter was looking at me and then she said, "Where is your daughter?" I said, "This is my daughter." My daughter was hugging me and her daughter hugged her. She gave me goose bumps. She touch at my heart and she made my eyes get fuller. And she said, "I'll be back next year." And I said, "So will I, God's will." I wanted to be in the parade. I was very happy and I was even proud of myself. I walked that parade and I'm talking in the streets we walked. I feel very happy and with Annie at my side, I feel much more happier. I had Annie's girlfriend with us too. If I have to do it, I'll do it all over again. You know something. When I left that parade, and when I was walking, these policemen—I don't know these policemen who they are, but these policemen they respected me. All of them asked me, "That's your daughter?" I said, "Yes." They said, "She's a very lucky young lady."

If I have the choice and somebody came to me and said would you prefer not to have Annie and have another child, I'd say no. I would have the same Annie. I'd rather have that same child. I'd rather have that same child over and over and over again. Annie's a very special child to me. She's a very, very, very special woman in my eyes. I love that little girl. I remember when Annie was born, I used to get up at nighttime and I used to look at Annie and I used to touch her face very nice and smooth. And I said, "Annie, I'll always love you and I'll always be there for you." And I will. As long as I'm alive, I'll be there for Annie. I always thank God. I say, "God, thank you for giving me this girl." I wouldn't change her for anything else in this world. This is a gift God gave me.

I'm not a gay woman but I feel lucky too, you know. I feel very lucky for having my daughter. That girl loves me so much too. She loves her mother, you know. I think it makes me stronger. That's all I can tell you. It just makes me a very strong person. I can go with Annie any place and it won't bother me. I experience more about it. I go to places that I never went for all the years I've been in New York. I'd never been in Chelsea. I'd never been in the Village. I never knew there was so many things was going on in the Village. Never been here Saturday night. It's a hot place to go. I really have to tell Annie. Sometimes I hold her and I kiss her, and I say, "Honey, thank you for showing me all these places." I say, "I was just a dumb broad in New York. I didn't know anything. Just go to work." I didn't know New York. I didn't know these places. At first, when she took me there, I couldn't believe what I'm seeing and I keep asking, "That's a woman? That's a man?" But now I know everybody. Now I knows all the faces.

Without Annie, I don't think about my life. I'm sorry, but I don't think about my life at all. I don't, you know. I only think about Annie's life. And when I think about Annie's life, I just want to know that Annie find somebody good and settle with that person. I know nothing lasts forever. Maybe when I was younger, I think everything lasts forever. But nothing lasts forever. And I would like it the best if Annie find somebody and she settle with that person before I die and then I know to myself, Annie have somebody. That that person would look out for Annie if Annie sick, God forbid. That person would take care of Annie. So I want to know Annie have somebody. Annie's a beautiful child. Annie have a lot to offer and I want to really know that when I'm dead and gone, that there is somebody there for Annie. Annie cries, she'll have a shoulder to cry on. Annie gets sad, that person can comfort Annie and say, "Annie, why you so sad? What happened to you?" I don't want that person to be me. Nobody could ever be me. I'm the only mother for Annie. But I want somebody to be there for her.

I'm gonna tell you something. Annie have a nice girlfriend, a very, very nice girlfriend. That girl, at first I did not like her at all. I did not like this girl for Annie. She's a pretty girl now, but something in that girl, I don't know. I never figure out why I feel this way about her. Maybe I didn't want nobody to come close to Annie. Gets me angry. Then, you know, that girl she makes me love her because she was a very nice girl. Very sweet, very polite to me. She used to come here and spend time with us. And then they broke up. When they broke up, it comes that she broke up with me too. I have to say that part. I feel like she broke up with me too. I used to treat that girl like she's my own child.

The only gay man I have known was Annie's friend. And his parents didn't care about him being gay, or I think they didn't know he was gay. I think that the mother alone knew he was gay. If the father knew he was gay, I think the father was going to kill him. But I knew my nephew was gay. But he commit suicide. My sister's son. He killed himself. When I met him he was about nineteen years old. From the first time I saw the kid, I knew he was gay. I knew my sister knew. If my sister didn't know her son was gay, something was wrong with her brains or her head. I don't know. But I didn't even know Annie was a lesbian yet. I knew my nephew was gay because this boy, he moved like a real girl. Dressed like a girl. Even talked like a girl. And his sisters even knew he was gay. I think his life was hard. The mother had love for him, but she never accept that boy for being gay. That's what really bothers me a lot. I still think about that kid. I think when he died he was about thirty years old when he committed suicide. And up to this day my sister never told me that boy was gay.

When I was in Trinidad, I'm gonna tell you they never said gay or lesbian. I'm gonna tell you the word they used to say. The word you would call them is faggot. You call them sissy and you would call the woman, she's a butch. That is an insult to call people that way. Say gay or lesbian. To me, I don't know. Maybe I'm wrong, but those words doesn't sound good in my ear. It really sounds terrible. That's the way I feel. Because if you read a book, it says my son is gay or my daughter is a lesbian. That's the way they would put it. I know even in the gay community they would say a butch. And that goes for faggot too. But I don't like those names. It gets me very, very angry. I prefer gay or lesbian. I used to wonder to myself, "Why do they say these things about these people? Why? Because this woman is having sex with this woman? Why do they care?"

But I never think about it growing up as a young woman. I never think about it. But when I came here, I never thought about it either until my daughter came out. Then I'm really think hard about it. I mean, I read books. We would go to different stores. She would take me, but I would choose my own book. What I like. I would read these books and I would read about some of these mothers. How they are bad to their children. When I came here,

I heard people from West Indies. They would tell me they would stone you down and they would kill you. Kill you. I said, "Why should they kill these people?" "Oh, because you know it's really terrible to be that way." I listen to my daughter a lot. And when people are against lesbians and gays, I don't know if it hurts me more than them, but it hurts me way down. Because then I put it in this way. "You're human. We all are human. Why you have to treat people like that?"

I met a young man last year when I went to the Gay Parade after I finished work. When I went there, I met this young guy from Trinidad. He tells me in New York he could do what he wants. He said, "I cannot do this in Trinidad. So many suicides in Trinidad. The young people commit suicide in Trinidad. They're killing themselves. You know when you gay in Trinidad, you know where they put you? In a mental institution. Yes. They take the children to see psychiatrists." This young man told us. He said, "You know how many psychiatrists I saw? I could be one." He said he could be a psychiatrist himself.

I'm gonna tell you something. Yes, there's something special about lesbians. A lot of love. And I think I even told Annie about it. With a man and a woman, the love can be good, the love can be strong. But there is something between two lesbians. The love is really strong. And you can see it in their face. Maybe I never been around a lot of men. Maybe I'm wrong. But this is something I see. These gay women. There is so much love, so much affection around them. How they will hold each other and they would kiss each other and caress each other. And I said, "God, are these people really real, or maybe just a put on?" It was not put on. It was real. If one go to the bathroom, the other one staying in front of the bathroom waiting for the other one to come out. When that one goes, they kiss each other. And I even told my own friend about it. I say, "You should try going with me one day with Annie to the lesbian place and you would see how different. There's so much love, it make you smile. It make you hop inside."

You think a man would ever treat a woman that nice? A woman will show a man love. He will show her love too. But there is something in him and he'll just push it aside. But a woman and a woman. I sit there and I was sipping a drink and I was looking all over. I watch how these women are so nice to the other one. Kissing. Leaning on them. Hugging them up. This is what you call love. You tell a man that and he would think you're a sick woman. He'd say, "You're crazy." That's what he would tell you. I'd just say, "Yeah. Let me take you to the Village."

Shirley, age fifty-six, was born in Trinidad and worked as a visiting nurse's aide. She identified herself as Catholic and had two children. An older daughter still lived in Trinidad. Shirley learned that her younger daughter Annie was a lesbian when she was eighteen in 1990. Shirley had attended PFLAG *meetings and marched in New York City Gay Pride parades. She lived in Brooklyn and was interviewed in 2000.*

18
Lois

WHATEVER KIND OF RELATIONSHIP HE WANTS
TO HAVE, WE WILL HAVE

ALISON REALLY WAS FAIRLY APPROPRIATE FOR A GIRL. Not that she liked to wear dresses. She certainly did not wear dresses often. She would much rather have worn slacks. She was active, but she was not a tomboy. Alison was more male in her refusal to accept authority and had she been a little boy when she was in school, the school would have been much more tolerant of her questioning authority. She really questioned authority. So I think if Alison had been outwardly male, school would have been easier, but because she wasn't her teachers would try and socialize her as a girl to be more compliant and that was not the case. But as far as physically, he did not like sports, still is not into sports. Certainly not coordinated. He often jokes about his lack of eye-hand coordination. But that's only in hindsight. I mean Alison really fell into the normal range of behavior for a little girl. Her behavior for a little girl was not unusual. Not typical, but not abnormal.

I had loads of fun with her. I felt very close to her. But I never felt that I was in tune with her on an emotional level. I felt in tune with her on an intellectual level. On things that she enjoyed. I felt very close to her that way. But I did not know really what she was about. And I did not know how to comfort her. Now, if it had been a son, I think I would have said, "Aw, he wants to comfort himself." Because society has that idea that men comfort themselves. They don't need to be comforted by hugging and holding. They need to just be reassured. I think then I might have felt closer that way, but because I couldn't comfort her the way I comforted my other daughter, I really felt out of place.

High school was really very hard. I do know that adolescence is very difficult and there is a lot of distance that goes on between parents and their child. Especially females. So some of what we were doing was normal and Alison would even attest to that. The saving grace for Alison then was that she was very bright and very talented musically. So she was very active in the band and made a name for herself that way because she was respected for her musical ability. So she had her little niche from time to time. She liked learning and would focus on that, so she had places from which to get comfort. But in hindsight, it was not enough. It's still really hard. We were very focused on her accomplishments and that embittered her too. Because she felt that she was only seen for her accomplishments, not for who she was. So it was a no win situation. It was really hard.

When she was a senior or maybe a junior, she asked to go to see a therapist which she did. Which pissed me off. Made me a bit furious. I think it was because at that time she was really sad and I just felt that I was missing something. I was not parenting this child right that she needed to go to a therapist. She felt like she was at the end of her rope and she said to me, "I feel like killing myself." I told her, "Don't joke about that. This is not a joke. It's not something that you ever say just to get someone's attention." She said, "I'm not joking." She never tried anything, but she was really very frustrated. At the end of her rope. She did go to see a therapist for about a month and she found it very, very helpful. Did a lot of work on what kind of schools to go to. Where she would feel more at peace and more comfortable. Decided that, yes, she'd much rather go to a big university where there was diversity and the place would be more accepting. She did look at sexual orientation, but at that time decided, no. She didn't think she was a lesbian. I just felt that I had failed.

High school was a lot of pressure. Cliquey. A lot of being forced to conform and Alison was not a conformist. Yet, she tried to conform. We used to joke that she would go through clothing changes and styles like the flavor of the week. Her friends were doing it too. This week I try this look, next week I try that look. Well it wasn't quite weekly. She went for the preppy look, then the punk look. I don't think that was the problem. I think in some ways the problem was certainly with the gender dysphoria and not even knowing that's what it was. If you don't know that you're a man, but you want to be able to relate to people that way, and society doesn't know it, you're confused and society is confused. So you don't even know why you're feeling this.

Maybe it was ten years ago. She, her name is now Evan, called us up and said, "I'm really very unhappy. I have what's called gender dysphoria." I said, "You've got to be kidding me." I think I just went numb. I heard what she was saying, but chose not to know what she was saying. I chose to believe that it would go away. My husband and I, we both found out together. He did the same thing. He just kind of thought it would go away. I tried to intellectualize it. I thought I can deal with this. I just need a lot of time.

I was absolutely thrown. My world fell apart. I had failed as a mother. My youngest child was in adolescence and had problems. So not only could I not raise my oldest child, I couldn't raise my youngest child well either. So, truly I entered into a crisis of motherhood. I loved being a wife and mother. That's what I wanted to do and I truly believed that I failed. I was scared and chronically depressed. Suicidal. I had to go therapy for seven years. It was not my children's fault. I had bought this belief system and was totally shattered by a society insistent that Mom has to do it well. And I didn't. I failed. Our marriage almost failed too. It didn't because we really battled hard. How my husband and I chose to deal with things was not always in synch. I'm a talker. He's not. I need to tell people things. He doesn't. We might not agree or understand, but we didn't try to change each other. It was important to both of us to try to keep the marriage stable. It was important to both of us to keep our children.

Then Alison told me that she was going to therapy. I was glad because that would straighten out what the dilemmas really were because I didn't know what else to think. I really didn't. I kind of just thought it would all go away. We knew it was happening, but I think perhaps we would have been happier to pretend that really nothing was happening to the body. It was just this external change and that this person is role playing. So Evan would be Evan, but she would still be Alison. But it's not role playing. Evan was trying to get us to see that it was not role playing. We went through a lot of numbness, but Evan wanted us to deal with it because we really weren't. I wanted to pretend it wasn't happening. Christine Jorgensen was the only person that I had known. And that was male to female. I did not know that there was any going from female to male.

It was clear to me that I was disintegrating and I wanted my family to understand why I was so strained. I told them about my younger daughter's problems and I told them about Evan. Evan wanted them to know. I felt they had to understand why I was like I was. Having had it thrown at me so much that I hadn't raised that child right. Another struggle was we didn't have the words to sum up what this transgender experience was. We grabbed whatever words we could so we used the metaphor of dying. Which really pissed Evan off. But it was the only thing that we had to grab on to. Alison has died. He said he hadn't, but to us she did and so we had a little bit of a battleground there. My relationship died. My mother-daughter relationship died.

I never had a son so I didn't know how I was going to relate to a son. Actually, I finally believed that I didn't have a mother-daughter relationship with Alison. Never really completely. We had what I thought was. But I really didn't. When I think back on my relationship with my other daughter, it really was very different. But I tried very hard to accept Alison for Alison. She was different. Okay, you're not going to do those mother-daughter things, but we did other really wonderful things. I have wonderful memories of this child. A neat person. Lots of good memories. When he used to wake up when he was a little kid, I'd think, "Good, another day with this kid."

What I learned is basically that you do X amount of therapy. You are in support groups where you are looking at these issues and then you dress and live as the opposite sex for a full year. After that, then you can start hormones. I don't think it's quite as rigid now, but back then it was really rigid. You needed to have two independent psychology evaluations. Then you get the hormones and Evan, being Evan, is very meticulous about these things. I mean, he always was being careful. For me, that was probably the most important thing. Knowing that he's following this procedure so carefully. Because I kept thinking, if this is wrong, it will become clear. Of course, I was also thinking and hoping this is wrong and it will become clear.

I remember my husband and I were having a hard time with Evan being angry. Furious with us. Enraged. I've seen it in other transgender individuals too. Some of it's adolescent separation. But the other is just this rage that nobody really understood me. I remember thinking he never could do anything right growing up. If you're not right with your body, people aren't dealing with you right. If you're not behaving the way they think you should be behaving because your body says you should be behaving this way—you're gonna feel that you're not doing anything right. And people are going to feel that you're not doing anything right either. So there's a lot of rage around that. Like Evan was saying, "You accept me not just now, but earlier. And you didn't, and so now I'm going to clobber you for not accepting me back then." I kept saying, "But I accepted you for what I believed you were. I believed you were a little girl. Why would I not believe that? We did the best we could."

We really learned a lot of tools for helping to separate parent and child, child and parent. It was then that I started to realize that I wasn't a failure. Just because I listened to my parents, it didn't mean that my child was going to. My parents were lucky. That was me. That's not all kids. I had to learn this. In fact, there is nothing I can do to actually make them do what I want. I could give them consequences if they didn't, but I couldn't make them do anything because there reaches a point where to make someone do something is truly physically abusive. I'm not going to beat my child. I'm going to give them consequences. We learned a lot of that. So that helped me to realize that there was nothing I could do to change Evan's decisions. Those are not my decisions to change. And those are her decisions. As painful as it was, they were gonna happen.

What really shocked me more than anything was that he chose the name Evan and not something like Alison. So I felt that he was rejecting something that I had given him and that Evan went from being Alison to Evan and from being female to male, and then from being Roman Catholic to Jewish and from heterosexual to homosexual. When he announced that he was becoming Jewish,

I lost it. Not really anything to do with being Jewish, but because that was the last thing. It was like now he has no reason to come home. Now mind you, we don't practice religion, but it was like he won't even come home for Christmas. There is no way for him to be connected to this family. But what I remember thinking was that I can't lose my connection to him. I'll send him a postcard. A very simple little thing. I am not going to lose my connection. Whatever level he will allow it, I will have it even if it's only post-cards. Whatever kind of relationship he wants to have, we will have. So it kind of improved for me because I let go.

I know the first two years were very much in keeping with the normal grief pattern. That first two years was so much dealing with logistics of—I don't have a daughter, I have a son. I don't have a she. I have a he. I don't have an Alison. I have an Evan. How do I go on with not having a daughter? What do I do with those memories? How do I talk about my infant that was a female to people that only know I have a son? So those first two years were very much like anybody who is grieving a loss. It's very logistical. It was probably at the end of that period when I started to send those postcards and saying whatever relationship I can have, that's what I will have. Even if it could only be in postcards or only on the phone, I will accept that and I will love that child that way. Then come to realize that the relationship between mother and child isn't dependent on him being a boy or a girl. It depends on him being a child and me being a mother. Well, it's not really that now. It's being an adult mom and an adult child and that's differ-ent. So then that's renegotiated again.

I've never really asked Evan a lot of questions. I very much believe that there needs to be boundaries between parents and child and I've told Evan to judiciously tell me things. He does. As the adult, I will not ask. I will ask if he feels all right. I will ask, if after the surgery, if it's healing. I do not want to see the surgery. Unless he wants me to see it or be there. I did not ask him a lot of questions about what makes him feel this way, or if something happened to him. I did ask if his father and I didn't fall into the typical male-female roles. I'm more likely to go outside and dig in the ground. I'm more likely to paint windows. He's more likely to be quiet and more cerebral, whereas, I'm still the tomboy. I asked if we confused him. He laughed. "No Mom. I'm not this way because you're that way. Trust me. There's nothing you did." Now I think one of the turning points was once when he walked down the stairs one summer and he had the hairiest man legs I'd ever seen and it threw me into shock. I don't know what I thought, but I never thought he was going to have hair on his legs. But he had man legs, and I think that was a moment that propelled me forward.

But after the surgery, I was terrified. Absolutely terrified that he would be killed. Absolutely. If anybody ever found out that she thought that she was a he. That she would suffer even after the surgery. And truthfully, now it's not a fear, but it's a concern. Evan passes very well for a man. But it could happen. Not because of anything that he does or doesn't do. I was also concerned about the long-term consequences of taking hormones. You don't know what happens when a human being has to take artificial hormones over the long haul. So that is a concern. But what would Evan's life be like without them? So, I'd rather he take the risk and take the hormones than to have him live his life in pretense.

You do start to see changes. Especially with a female. The beard starts fairly quick and in Evan's case, because he was only twenty, he hadn't really fully formed as a female. This was really wonderful for him because his body physique is much more male. His partner is also a FTM, but he was older when he transitioned so you see subtle things that will never disappear. His hips are female, whereas, Evan's quite male. Really the hormones were able to really stop a lot of things. So he's quite male. Actually, the first time that we saw him in full male exterior—not dressing as a male and pretending to be a male and living this life as male, but on hormones with facial hair and after surgery—was at a family reunion. Our family was remarkable. Absolutely remarkable. I think because my husband and I made it very clear that this is our child and it will always be our child. If we didn't know what the hell we were doing, we certainly weren't going to tolerate any of them worrying about it. So if they didn't approve, tough. Just don't show it when we're around. I think that was part of it and the other part was that we are blessed with a very accepting family.

How do I explain him? I now really believe that gender and sexuality are interconnected, but distinctly different. I believe that sexuality is very much on a sliding scale from heterosexual to homosexual to non sexual. I'm not quite sure what non sexual is, but that's how I would draw it because people have varying degrees of sexuality. I've also come to believe that, in the course of a lifetime, that line can shift for some people and that with sexuality sometimes you can believe that you are one thing and then later on realize that no, I'm really not. With sexuality, I don't know if it's biological, or genetic or hormonal, but I do think there is certainly some biological aspect. With gender, I see it very much on a sliding scale from being born male or female and staying male or female—to being born male, but moving to female—or born male moving to female. I don't think it's because there is a genetic defect. I just think that the coding is different. We haven't gotten it all straightened out, but I also think hormones in utero are very important. We haven't gotten that all straightened out either.

I would say that the essential difference is his inner sense of peace. Like there's less anxiety in him. He's both changed and not changed. He certainly does things that he didn't do as Alison. But yet, he still does do things like Alison. It's just that now when I look at him, it's in a different context because he's Evan. But I can remember Alison sitting with a dress on like this. The way you would with pants on, but with a dress on or skirt. I used to tell him that he was not supposed to sit that way. We don't do that. We do this. Body language, you know. Things are more in keeping with what I'm seeing. Yeah, he's got a beard and yeah, he's got a receding hairline and he's got hairy legs, but he still likes the same things. He still has the same kinds of belief systems.

Personally, I've come to think it doesn't really much matter. If you feel you're A, then it's A. If you tell me that you feel that you are gay, you're gay. If you tell me you want to be gay, then you're gay. If you tell me you're a male and you present as a male, then you are male. You could dress like a male. You can walk around like a male. Women theoretically can do what males do. But no, you don't get treated like a male if you're not a male. And no, you can't do what males can do. You don't want to pretend to be male. If you're male, you want to be male.

Lois, age fifty-five, was married, and had worked as an art the rapist. She had two children. Her oldest child, Alison—now Evan—had been married and disclosed that he planned to transition to male at age twenty in 1987. He was now married to another FTM trans man and identified as a gay male. Lois had been active in the civil rights movement. She was an activist in the trans community and an active member of PFLAG, helping other parents in their struggle to accept a trans child. She lived in New Jersey and was interviewed in 2000.

19

Eleanor

IF YOU CAN'T BE SUPPORTIVE, DON'T BE AROUND

I THINK I WAS CLOSE TO HER, but she was a very difficult child. Right from the beginning she was a real handful growing up. There was a big difference between my two kids. She was a very active baby even before birth. My first, her brother, was a very placid child and it felt as though I could do nothing wrong. With Catherine, it felt as though I could do nothing right. She was just contrary. Like at age two, I would say, "Would you like toast or English muffin for your breakfast this morning?" "English muffin with butter please." "Here it is." "Oh, I don't want any butter. I won't eat it. It has butter on it." "Well, I'm sorry, that's what I fixed. That's what you asked for." She was opinionated and contrary and oppositional right into adolescence and she's still the same kind of person. She and my husband are rather similar in this regard and had a hard time getting along. It's very difficult and sometimes it felt as though I were in the middle and even having to choose between her and him. Being put in a place where you have to choose between your husband and your daughter is no fun.

I knew something was wrong, but Catherine wouldn't tell me why. I did know that a friend of hers had just cut her out of her life and that she was just devastated. I said to her, "You're miserable. You're not doing well in school. Obviously something is wrong." What she said was that this girl asked her if she ever thought she could love a woman or something like that. Catherine told her that yes she had, but thought that most people had those feelings. Then this friend said she thought she was a lesbian and was never going to speak to her again. I was very sympathetic and

168

urged her to go to the school counselor. But she said she didn't think it was true.

Now even before this, she had been active in the Gay-Straight Alliance at school. But I didn't think anything of it because as Unitarian Universalists, we're very pro-diversity and accept people as they are. I did know a few gay people. Not many, but there was a course at church on understanding gays and lesbians and that did more than anything else to put me in an accepting frame of mind. In any case, while working with this school counselor, Catherine finally decided that maybe she was lesbian. It took about four or five months and I was part of it at every step of the way. I did say to her that I guessed it meant she would never have a traditional wedding and a family and that was a disappointment. But she told me that she still might like children. I said, "Well, gay people have children and if you find yourself in the future having or wanting a child, I'll certainly help if I'm in a position to be able to help." And she thought that was very nice.

At the end of a year and a half of college she decided to drop out and move out west with her then girlfriend. I didn't think it was a great idea, but I didn't tell her she couldn't. That doesn't work. Not with her. I didn't see her nearly as much, but I did still visit about three times a year and spent long weekends with her. So we were still reasonably close and we did e-mail a lot and telephoned. I knew she had been dressing in men's clothing. I thought if that's the way she wanted to present herself, it was fine. She had gotten her eyebrow pierced and she had a thing in her tongue and so this was just another aspect of self-expression as far as I was concerned.

So, anyway, a year ago when I was out there, she said that she was starting testosterone and she had had some counseling with somebody who had signed something that said that this was an okay way for her to go. She just said that she had always felt that she was living in the wrong body and that she was scheduling a mastectomy which was a big surprise. Looking back, I mean after she told me, I did see things. I mean, at age four, when we went shopping for some dress-up clothes, she said she wanted a white shirt and a sport coat and a tie. Those were the days when you still dressed up to go to church, and for years she would wear sport coats and white shirts and ties. At the time I didn't think anything of it because she was very fond of her brother and so I thought this was a way to be like him. I'm a fairly easygoing person and none of this had any kind of disastrous effect on me and it didn't worry me as far as her gender identity. The fact that she wanted to wear pants was fine. She didn't look good in a skirt anyway.

Well, I guess I felt disappointment that I wasn't going to have a daughter like I thought I was. I'm my mother's only daughter. I have three brothers. My mother and I were very close and I felt a loss that I wouldn't have the same kind of relationship with her that my mother and I had. She helped me when each of the kids was born and we would do house decorating together and found that we could do things for each other that neither one of us could do alone. Like painting a room or going through pictures, or something that you couldn't face on your own. My mother died this year and it's been really hard. So I had to give up the idea that I would have that kind of relationship with a daughter. But maybe it's more because of who she is. But it is like grieving. For the loss of the person that was, or that I thought would be, and this new person that was somebody I didn't know very well. I had a lot of education to go through and Catherine was very helpful about saying what to read and bringing me along.

I did some reading on the Web and there was this name of a person, Harry Benjamin, with whom the protocol of transition is associated. Most people go through an extensive amount of therapy and are supposed to live or pass as the opposite gender for a year at least. Now Connor, that's his new name, didn't. The key thing for some of the people that I met at his transgender support group seemed to be which restroom did they use when in public places. I never asked, but I think Connor continued to use—at least at work—the women's room. If she used a men's room early on, I don't know.

But certainly she looked very androgynous and she dressed in men's clothing. But if you looked closely, you could see that she was female. So what counted as a year of passing, I don't know. But she short-circuited the amount of counseling that the Harry Benjamin protocol called for. She had gone to a transgender counselor and he just felt that the amount of counseling recommended wasn't really needed and was willing to sign whatever had to be signed so Connor could get testosterone. She didn't tell me exactly how long she was in counseling, but I'm sure that it wasn't that long.

I had a lot of questions and we did a lot of e-mailing and Internet chat sessions during that time. She was pretty good about answering my questions, but basically I came to the conclusion that if I didn't accept—well at one point she said that if I couldn't be supportive, she didn't want me around and unsupportive. I guess she felt I was asking too many questions and I wasn't being supportive enough. It doesn't leave me a lot of room. And since I obviously wanted to continue our relationship, I felt I better be supportive. Now that was the kind of behavior that I experienced all her growing up years. The impression is that Connor doesn't need opposition. That's what he said. "If you can't be supportive, don't be around." When she had told me she was transgender and was going to have a mastectomy, I had said, "Gosh, this is a really big step and irreversible. Are you sure you really want to do that?" That was one of the times when I got told to stop questioning so much.

My husband doesn't see her nearly as often as I do. When I go to visit her, he doesn't go. Well, theoretically he accepts, but I think that it will be a long time before he accepts her as a him emotionally. I don't think it's really real for him the way it is for me. He won't call him Connor, his new name, and he won't refer to him as he. He says she still looks and sounds like a female to him. In denial, I guess. My son is fine with it. He was married last year and asked Connor to be a part of the wedding party. It was just before she transitioned and she said she would if she didn't have to wear a dress. So she was one of his attendants and wore a tux. When Connor told me about the tux, I said that she needed to write a letter to all the people, her whole mailing list and mine, and let them know because the last thing she should want was for her to upstage her brother's wedding. I said, "You don't want the transition to take center stage at the wedding. That wouldn't be right." And she agreed. She wrote a wonderful letter and people who got it commented on how well-written it was. So everybody knew. The only adverse response was from one of my mother's sisters. Like my husband, the lesbianism was fine, but not the transgender issue. Catherine's girlfriend couldn't deal with it either, but he has met another woman who self-identifies as lesbian and they're doing some work on continuing the relationship because when he transitioned to male, it changed her self-image.

I eventually came to the conclusion that lesbianism or homosexuality is either genetic or there's some physical basis for it. There are some differences since she transitioned, but there are more similarities than I expected there would be. She's still my daughter in some ways, but just a male version. More self-assertive and more self-confident. Seemingly more at peace. There's been a reduction in the combativeness. It's less than it used to be. Whether that's sort of a maturation or whether that's being more at one with who you are, I don't know. But then Connor lives out west and so I don't see her. I mean I don't see him as often. I'm not as involved in his life. So no, we don't relate the same, but as to cause and effect, well I think the differences in the way we relate are more age-related and distance-related and independence-related than they are gender-related.

You remember the '70s, that free-spirit kind of times. I was just ahead of the flower-power type of stuff and so I was not the kind of free-spirit who was experimenting with drugs. I had a kind of a straight upbringing and straight experiences through college and graduate school. But it did influence how I thought. So I was a pretty laid-back mother and with my son that worked fine because he was a laid-back kid. But with Connor, I think I should have set more limits. I let them both do what they wanted when they wanted, but not to the extent that it interfered with getting things accomplished. My father was very much of the philosophy that when a kid is ready to do something, they'll do it and if you push them too soon or if you hold them back, that doesn't do the kid any favors. I really had that kind of model for parenting. I think that it works well with some children and not well with others. I don't think it was a good model for Connor, for her personality. So, looking back, I think that if I had known how to set more limits and given her a more structured life, it probably would have been better for her.

I think I have much more of a chance of maintaining the kind of relationship that I want with Connor and looking back, it seems like it's more constant than I anticipated that it would be. We've had more visits back and forth over the last year than in the year or two prior. But part of that was the wedding stuff and also my mother's death. His friends are primarily in the gay and the transgender community and they're very accepting of me. They have all sorts of questions about how did I get to be as accepting as I am and so they obviously want to apply it to their own parents. I say it's my Unitarian Universalist background. I think it is. I really do. I think it's partly my personality and I think it's partly my beliefs. I don't understand how parents can reject their own children. It doesn't make sense to me. I think that the more people have experience with out lesbians or out transgenders, the better off society will be in terms of acceptance. Now, how militant lesbians or homosexuals or transgenders should be in terms of getting what they think they should have, that's a whole other issue. Cheney has a daughter who is homosexual and the more that that continues to happen, I think the better off we'll all be.

I have the feeling that they really look at me with some wonder. Here's a mom who is accepting and a nice person. Some of his friends and I exchange e-mail letters sometimes and then when I go and see them, they seem genuinely happy to see me which is nice. I'm so much more aware of that population and the issues that they face and I'm meeting a whole group of people that I would not have met under other circumstances. They are a great bunch of people and very supportive of each other. A lot of them don't have support from their own families. So when they met me and I was supportive, they kind of adopted me. Everyone there wants me to be their mother.

Eleanor, age fifty-six, was married and a retired librarian. She had two children and identified herself as Unitarian. Her child Catherine— now Connor—came out as a lesbian at age seventeen and then as transgender at age twenty-two in 1999. Eleanor called herself a feminist and had been active in the environmental movement. She lived in Pennsylvania and was interviewed in 2001.

20

Annemarie

YOU CAN'T HIDE A BABY

I THINK I SORT OF EXPECTED IT when my daughter Bonnie told me. I felt mostly relief that she wasn't in any real major trouble like with the law or something like that. It wasn't a big blow to me. In high school she was mostly with girls. She very seldom had anything to do with the opposite sex and she did begin to question it herself. She would say she wasn't really sure and I didn't want to push it because, like most mothers, you really think maybe it's a stage they'll outgrow. It's not that I didn't want to ask her. It was just one of those things that I wasn't really sure I wanted to hear a positive answer. But she didn't tell me until she was just about ready to graduate college. All her friends were for the most part lesbian. Her roommate was also a lesbian. So I knew she was before she told me. She would tell me she was going to bring this one home for a weekend. No problem, because I'm open to accept almost anybody unless they show me I cannot trust them for some reason. But the girls were all lovely that she brought home. Even in high school.

My feelings? Well, it was like putting away dreams of grandchildren or a normal husband. Your child getting married normally. The husband-wife type thing was gone. But obviously, she was never going to get married normally to a man. That was a disappointment. But I've always felt that both my daughter's happiness was more important than what I wanted. I've always let them live their lives the way they want. Actually, my first question was, "You're not gonna get AIDS, are you?" "No," she said. "The chance of women getting AIDS is a lot less than men and I got myself tested and I don't have it." Then she said that she wasn't going to tell her father until after he paid the last semester of tuition. So, I said, "All right." No way I wasn't going to support her.

Her father didn't know. He's a good person, but he's always had a problem with gay people. She knew I was upset and said to me, "There's PFLAG, you know." But I was nowhere near ready to go near PFLAG. Maybe it was a sense of shame or something. It wasn't right. You know that your daughter isn't quite right and I was really not ready to face anybody else with it. But after I stayed around the house like six months to acclimate myself to the idea and got accustomed to it, I said to her, "Well, maybe we'll go." She said, "Okay, we'll tell Dad we're going shopping." Rather than lie to my husband, I told him and, lo and behold, he says that he'll come with me. I was shocked. Well, we went to PFLAG. At first, we went regularly for support, but now I don't need it. It took him a while.

He loves his daughter very much, but it went against all the principles that he was ever brought up with about right and wrong. Being a lesbian was definitely wrong. But, his love for his daughter overcame any negative feelings and while he still is not really all that happy with it, he's accepted it as much as he can. That she's gay. That she had a partner. A woman. The only thing that really bothers me is that I share Matthew Shepard's mother's worry. I mean, her nightmare. What happened to her son is my nightmare. That somebody will turn on my daughter and do to her what happened to Matthew Shepard. It's the safety thing. Last Christmas I gave her one of those motion detectors, a garage door opener. I didn't want her to have to stop and open the garage door. For safety. But other than that, she has a good life like anybody else. A normal life.

Then last year when I was at the doctor's, lo and behold, out from another set of doors comes Bonnie. I said, "What are you doing here?" She said, "What are you doing here?" "Never mind, what I'm doing here. You just tell me what you're doing here." She looks at me and says, "Just calm down. I think I'm pregnant and I'll know this afternoon." All the way home, my husband and I look at each other and go, "We're going to be grandparents! We're going to be grandparents!" There was no father. The husband was artificial insemination. They have no idea of who he is except for the medical history. I knew that they had wanted a baby. In fact, her partner had tried twice, but I never expected it would be Bonnie. She just didn't seem the type that would be a mother. Then she called to tell me she was pregnant and when we got off the phone, we started yelling again, "We're going to be grandparents!" It was the longest pregnancy I ever went through and then she was born. A beautiful baby girl.

Because it was a biological, a blood child, it was like our grandchild. I did go back to PFLAG because other parents are grandparents and so I knew they'd understand how I felt. And they did. The PFLAG people, they all thought it was marvelous, absolutely wonderful. I've always liked PFLAG because listening to people who also have gay children doesn't make you feel so odd or alone anymore. PFLAG gave me and my husband support. That we are not oddities. Other people who are in our position understand how we feel and they were tremendous. Sometimes they talk about that something maybe went wrong inside of them that made their child that way. But I never thought like that. I'm still a Catholic, but I do not care for the church's position on this at all. I think they're hypocrites. As far as I'm concerned, they are way off the mark. They are way off the mark on a lot of other things too, but that does not affect my faith. The fact that I'm a Catholic does not have anything to do with the fact that I could accept my daughter as gay.

Maybe you can try to hide the fact that your daughter's a lesbian, but you can't hide a baby. So we told people. About Bonnie being a lesbian and that she was going to be a mother. My sister had a hard time accepting it, but I didn't push it. There's no point in it. Her two daughters thought it was marvelous. A new cousin. My husband's family thought it was wonderful because it would be a blood grandchild and he would have his very own grandchild like his sisters and brothers. I told my aunt that she was going to become a great-great aunt. Her mouth dropped open and when she shut it, I said, "You know Bonnie is a lesbian." She said, "Yes, I know because Bonnie was on television on one of those shows that was about lesbians and I saw her, but I didn't know whether to call you, or what. Nobody ever said anything about it so I kept my mouth shut." That was two years before Bonnie was pregnant.

My parents brought us up to have manners and don't answer back and all that. But they never told us you must be this, or you must do that and I wouldn't do that to my kids either. I believed they should follow their own dreams because they have their lives to live like I'm living mine doing the work I do. I'm allowed to fulfill my dream. I'm letting my girls do the same. Because everybody's an individual and I see no reason to force a dream on to my child. I said to them, "Don't ever let me see you in court." And I never did. They were good kids. They decided early on, both of them, that they wanted to be somebody. Well, you can't be somebody and be strung out on drugs. If you have a child too early, before you're ready for it, then you can't do what you want to do. They were careful and are now doing what they want to do. This idea of being somebody was their main thing.

I was slightly over-protective. We had our go-rounds. Bonnie screaming for me to get out of her face. She was a very outgoing child. She was not afraid of anything. Put her in a playpen. No way. She was the one who climbed on top of the refrigerator. She was the one who when we had the jungle gym outside would go hand over hand over the top. She'd see boys playing touch football, and I thought, "Oh, what's next?" I regret that I was over-protective. I should have let them go. Have more faith in them. The one thing, if I could do it over, would to be much more relaxed. But I brought them up the best way I could. To be independent people and make a contribution to society.

My sister said that one of her elementary school pupils had just gone through a trauma because his parents were breaking up because his mother was a lesbian and was going to live with her partner. I said to my sister that the baby won't have that because she'll never know the father, so she hasn't lost anything. She'll always know just Bonnie and her partner, so there won't be that problem. My sister feels that as long as gay wasn't being pushed on her or rammed down her throat, it was okay. Like some of the gay people I have seen have to tell you, "I'm gay, you know, and what are you going to do about it?" My daughter and her partner were never like that. She didn't ever bring it up and her partner was always included in family occasions. They never pushed gay so you saw them as individuals rather than like a gay couple falling all over each other at every opportunity. I have seen that at my daughter's house when she's had parties and I think it would be just as embarrassing if they were heterosexual. Keep it private is how I look at it. Don't put it in my face.

My daughter would be my daughter no matter what she was. No matter. I love my kids. They will always be my kids and I accepted them unconditionally. There are all kinds of parents. But I would never throw my daughter out on the street because she was a lesbian. Absolutely not. She would always have a place to stay here. I'm involved with the baby as much as they let me. If they need me, I'm there and I have been helping take care of her so we have had the chance to see her grow up. A chance that we never would have had if we hadn't accepted Bonnie. When the baby was born and my family saw her and held her and saw how good and adorable she was, they all, including my sister, had a change of heart. They're all much more accepting now. My family is not always easy and we've had our hard times, especially with Bonnie being a lesbian. But our grandchild is now eight months and she healed us. She healed our family.

Annemarie, age sixty, was married, and had a Master's degree in library science. She worked as a home health aide and identified herself as Catholic. Annemarie had two children and was a member of PFLAG. Her daughter Bonnie disclosed that she was a lesbian at age twenty-one in 1989 and at the time of the interview had an eight month old baby daughter. Annemarie lived in Connecticut and was interviewed in 2001.

21

Lillian

MY CHILD IS NOT AN ABOMINATION

I'M JUST AN ORDINARY MOTHER of six children, three boys and three girls. I was very active in their school life. I knew what was going on every minute of every day with these kids. I was at their schools as much as they were. At least, when they were young before I had to work so much. My house was always open to their friends so I didn't have to worry about where they were. There were always lots of girls, particularly with my two daughters, Kim and Janice. They were, you might say, a gang. Six or eight of them. Always together. But I never thought anything of it. They were just girls who were not particularly interested in boys. They all went to the ball games. They went partying together. They went everywhere together. They liked doing their own thing.

I found out about Kim before I found out about Janice. Kim had moved out as soon as she graduated from high school and I realized later that she was living with someone who was gay. I didn't associate that with her at that time until she took off to go to California with an openly gay girl. It was then she told me that she was gay. How did I feel when she told me? Disbelief, hopeless, helplessness. What did I do wrong? How could this happen to my beautiful girl? All of the emotions that you can possibly imagine. But I am a fairly educated person and I believe that things happen for a reason so I started doing some research. I found out how many young lesbian women were turned away from their families and they had no place to go. But I still didn't know about my other daughter, Janice. She had been away from home for eight years and she told me when she knew that I was going to be visiting her.

I loved my daughters dearly and I knew that to have a relationship with them, I had to accept their lifestyle for what it was. Their lifestyle. Not mine. Not my choice for them, but this is what they had chosen to do with their lives. I wondered how a person becomes gay. Through what I have researched, most of them say it's a matter of genetics. I didn't have anything to do with it. It wasn't my choice for them to have this lifestyle. I learned many years ago, after the fact, that Janice's father had attempted to sexually molest her. She was able to get out of it because she was old enough to know what was going on. It was kept from me. I was not at home and I never had the slightest inkling of anything like this going on. For a while I wondered if this had anything to do with it. I still wonder to this day. Her father died two years before Janice told me that she was a lesbian. If he knew, we never discussed it so I don't know how he felt.

It was really hard with both my daughters. But I had learned because of Kim, my first daughter, that for me to have a relationship with my child, I also had to have a relationship with her partner. I was successful because I grew to like her partner very much. I didn't understand it. I didn't approve. But to keep the relationship, I had to accept. When Janice told me, it was just a matter of me accepting what I already knew. Of course, again my feelings were of sadness. Such wasted opportunities to have what we call a normal family life. But I respected my daughter and I wanted her to do what made her happy. She has recently separated from her partner of fifteen years and that was very hard for her. It was probably basically on the same order as getting a divorce and she has now kind of put her life back together. She is in a new relationship and I don't know where this one will go, but we will see what happens. Two lesbian daughters! But they are happy. And if they're happy, that makes me happy.

Their brothers and sisters, they were in on it from the beginning. I think even before me. We are a close knit family and it made no difference to them. They respect their lifestyle. I've told all my sisters, but they all love my children so it made no difference to them. I have no problem telling people that I have two daughters who are gay. I'm a very independent person. I've always said they could either accept it or not. It doesn't matter to me one way or the other because it's not going to change my attitude towards my children.

But I had concerns about them being mistreated. I do pick and choose who I tell because I know there are people, opinionated people out there who would not understand what it's like. It hurts when I hear people make remarks about faggots or lesbies. It bothers me, but I say nothing. On several occasions I have been asked to sign a petition for gays and lesbian rights and I will sign anything I'm asked to sign. I don't know if I would change anything. We always say, if we could go back and change it, we would. But I'm not real sure that I would. I did the very best I could under very difficult circumstances. They were all little at the same time. They all grew up and lived at home at the same time. There was one older boy, then three girls, and then two boys. They all had a taste of growing up in a home where the father drank too much and the mother had to work too much. But I think, overall, it was still a happy home and the relationship between all of them was always good. So I don't think that I would change anything.

I have always considered myself very open-minded, but I will confess that in the past I have wondered how parents react when they realize they had a lesbian child. I have known people who have turned away from their child when they told them that they were gay. I think it's a shame and a disgrace. Your child is a part of you and will always be a part of you so therefore, it's up to you to understand what your child is going through and what she needs. I have known gay people. I have had friends that were gay and I've tried to accept them as I would accept anyone. My view on homosexuality now is not any different than it was to begin with. I think probably my research helped me to know that I could accept anyone for their lifestyle. Their lifestyle has nothing to do with my lifestyle. Therefore, we are two separate entities and we can live in the same world and do our own thing. My reward is that they know that I support them and will be there for them.

My beliefs and opinions on homosexuality are live and let live. As long as it doesn't cross over the bounds into my territory. My territory being that of my sex life. I would not want to be approached for any sexual activity by a lesbian and I would not offer any male companionship to a lesbian. I would like to further understand how one daughter in the same family, raised by the same set of parents, could get married and have a family—and then two more choose the lesbian way. I would like some answers to that, but I'm not sure that I'll ever get them.

I don't think my reaction would be any different with a gay son. I would accept him and his partner as I have accepted my daughters and their partners. I don't know if my experience would have been different had I known about it when they were teenagers. Maybe I would have done the research earlier and tried to talk to them about it. Of course, they didn't tell me anything was going on those years so I knew nothing about it. I really knew nothing about lesbianism other than what I had read in books. As far as my religious beliefs, I have not discussed this with anyone in my church because my church quotes from the bible that lesbianism is an abomination. Kim and Janice are my children and they are human beings and children of God. Maybe they don't act like other people in terms of their sex life, but they have reached the age of adulthood and can do what they want. My children are not an abomination.

Lillian, age sixty-six, lived in Texas and was a widow. She attended college and worked in human services. She had six children. Her first daughter, Kim, told her that she was a lesbian at age twenty-seven in 1984 and Lillian learned that a second daughter, Janice, was a lesbian eight years later in 1992. Lillian identified as Protestant and was affiliated with a fundamentalist church that taught that homosexuality was a sin. She was interviewed by mail in 2001.

ACTIVISM

22
Marie

SHE MADE ME MORE OF A PERSON

I 'M SITTING ON THE FRONT STEPS of my house when my daughter Angie sat down next to me and said, "I have something to tell you. Mom, I'm gay." I said, "What!" She said, "I'm gay." I said, "Oh, Okay." I really had no idea what that meant. Of course, I knew that being gay or being a lesbian was a woman caring for another woman, but I couldn't actually understand what she was saying. I was unable to digest it. Maybe it was because she took me by surprise. I really didn't have any information to know what it meant. So I didn't react to it. It was a shock, a total shock. I was not prepared to handle it. It never occurred to me that my daughter would be gay. I mean she had gone out with boys.

Then I started to think about it and the more I thought about it, the more I became out of control. I couldn't understand why she would be gay. What did she mean? What did I do wrong? I thought that being gay was a woman that didn't want to be a woman. I don't know where I got this information, but that was my idea of what a lesbian was. A woman that didn't want to be a woman. Didn't want to get married. Didn't want to have children. Didn't want to identify herself in the female role. So I thought that my daughter must not want to be like me. Have children and get married, the way I did.

So everything was completely out of proportion, having no information and no one that I could turn to for information. This was long before PFLAG was ever in existence. I never knew a gay person. I never had a relative that I knew was gay. I never thought about it. So I started to go crazy. I became very nervous, very depressed, and very angry. She was living at home and would go out late at night and not return until the wee hours of the morning. I couldn't reason or talk to her. She was getting completely out of control and wouldn't adhere to any of the rules that I had set up. I did find out that she was seeing a woman who was married. I waited up for her one night to be dropped off and I jumped out of the house like a crazy person in front of the car. I confronted her and we had one battle after another. She realized that she couldn't live at home and be who she was if I was going to be a lunatic. So she moved out. She was seventeen. It was maybe 1976.

She used to call me on the phone, but I just couldn't speak to her. I didn't know what to say. I would get so choked up that I could hardly communicate. In the meanwhile, she saw her sister who used to go visit her behind my back. It was a terrible situation. My husband and I suffered through this. He was not supportive at all. He didn't see why I couldn't understand that she was the same person she always was. It was just her sexuality. My husband oversimplified it. I mean this was her life. She was choosing a life that I didn't understand and it created a tremendous barrier between us. My husband has this personality of minimizing serious situations. I would like to say that it's because he was not her biological father, but he has been as much a father to her as he has to his own natural daughters. His experience was not mine. He was in pain because I inflicted pain upon him by having it affect our relationship. But he didn't feel the shame or the disappointment I was feeling. The anger that I was feeling. He just was not there for me and our marriage suffered. There was no question, I handled it poorly.

My mother found out about it. She was there when I flared up and did some kind of wild crazy thing like trying to get into my car and kill myself. I don't know that I would have killed myself, but that's how I was feeling at that moment. My mother didn't know why I was going nuts and so she was really one of the first people I told. But she was convinced Angie was going through a stage and that she would change. My mother never really accepted it. Then my brother found out about it and decided that she needed psychiatric care. You have to remember how many years ago this was. She did go to a woman therapist for about a year who told her that there was nothing wrong with her. That it was us who had the problem. Of course, I thought the therapist might be nuts too because that kind of thinking was unheard of in those days.

I felt shame. Shame that my daughter was not like other people's children. I always wanted my daughter to be perfect. I wanted her to be wonderful. I wanted her to be smart and accepted socially. I wanted to be proud of her and see her get married and have children. All the things that I had dreamed for her—here again—always thinking of myself. Well, my bubble was burst and I just couldn't handle it. Oh my God! When I think of what she must have gone through and how I had no idea.

What really changed my thinking was that I met a woman who was a lesbian who had left her husband for a woman. They're still together and just celebrated their twenty-fifth anniversary. I confided in her and she began to raise my consciousness. We were both going through a terrible time. She with her husband, and me with coming to terms with my daughter. I got a lot of information from her about being a woman that was in love with another woman. It took me a lot of years. Most people take maybe one, two, three years. Me, it took ten. I'm really disappointed in myself that it took me so long. But time helped. I was missing my daughter. I wanted to have a relationship with her on whatever terms it had to be. I just didn't know how to go about it. I didn't know what to do. It seemed like I would never be able to feel comfortable with the fact that my daughter was gay.

This lesbian friend of mine was a major turning point. She was very politically active and at one point told me that I was really at a place where I could be helping other people. She pushed me to go to PFLAG. I thought, "What the hell. I'll go to a meeting and see what it's about." That was around five or six years ago. Going to meetings really helped. I needed support. I needed validation. I needed someone to hold me and tell me they knew my pain. This is what I do for other mothers. For people that I don't even know. I'll hold them and let them cry. Let them free themselves of the pain that we need to get rid of. Experience it. Get through it. I wasn't allowed to feel it. I mean my husband was saying to me, "I don't understand why you can't deal with it. She's the same person she was. She's just a lesbian." It was more than that to me. I needed someone to say how very painful it was for me. How hard it was for me to accept. I didn't care what she was going through. I had no idea and I didn't give a damn! I only knew that it was causing me pain. That's where I was at that time.

It was a very slow process. She started to come around and visit. We had our difficulties. But now she's marvelous. She's so fantastic. She's kind and she's caring and she's giving and loving. She's more than I could ever have hoped for as a daughter. I'm so proud of her. She's perfectly comfortable with the fact that she's gay. There's no question about it. She's not at all flamboyant, like I'm gay and I'm in your face. Because I know lesbians that are like that. Take the Gay Pride March. There are people that march that go bare breasted with nipple rings and all kinds of really outrageous stuff. Of course, the media always focuses on them and not the people that are just ordinary people. So they give this impression that people who are gay or lesbian are nuts and there's something wrong with them if they have to behave that way. That's not true. Because that's the way these people choose to express themselves. And being accepting means accepting how people express themselves as long as they're not hurting anybody. I consider them a radical part of the movement and they play a necessary role as far as I'm concerned. See what a long way I've come.

I'm sorry for the pain I caused her. But when I think of what we've gone through together and where it has brought us, I can't think about the past. To me the past is the past. She's in a relationship and we never even think twice about her not being with this partner of hers. We're completely accepting of who she wants in her life. We are very, very open about it. We feel that the rest of our family needs to be accepting, or don't even bother including us in your plans. If they don't like it, it's their problem. She's enriched our whole family. Our extended family too. Even my in-laws. We've raised everyone's consciousness.

My daughter knew that she was not going to get married and have children the conventional way. But she wanted to have kids and be a mother. I felt pretty damn good about that. Some people hate their mothers so much they never want to have a kid. So maybe she didn't have a bad experience with me as her mother because she wanted to be a mother too. So we talked about it and I had never heard of donor insemination. She said, "Mom, I'd really like to have a baby and I really can't do this on my own. Do you think that you could help me take care of the baby if I go through with this?" So I agreed that I would help her.

We talked about donor insemination and what it meant and everything that was involved. She went to a sperm bank and did the research and checked out all the donors and their history. She wanted someone intelligent and the donor's father, I think, is a doctor and comes from an Italian background. She wanted some similarities in the genetic structure. She also felt that she didn't want anyone to indicate any interest somewhere down the line. She wanted total responsibility for this child. I went with her to be inseminated on several occasions. It took her not too long, maybe six months, to get pregnant. This was going to be my first grandchild and it was a wonderful experience. Every little thing whether it was the pregnancy tests, finding out she was pregnant, or morning sickness. I was in the hospital when the baby was born and it was joyous. Absolutely joyous! So she had this little angel boy and I helped take care of him the first two years of his life. And my daughter is an absolutely marvelous mother.

When we discussed her pregnancy, we decided that the way that we responded to it was the way that other people were going to and that we would not give them permission to make us feel uncomfortable or unhappy about it. We were not ashamed of it. When we told other people, family members, we surmised that they probably talked a great deal about us behind our backs. They're old fashioned and conventional and this was unheard of. But we really didn't care. It wasn't going to interrupt our happiness. But it brought our family closer when we had this baby. It was a gift. The interesting thing was that our family behaved the way we wanted. We set the ground rules. Now she has a second child. Another boy.

I have some concerns. My major concern for these children is that they, at some point, will understand that they are donor inseminated and that they have a biological father, but an unknown father. There may be a certain amount of resentment as they get bigger. The older boy has already shown signs of difficulty and has told his mother that he doesn't want her to be a lesbian. He wants her to get married because he wants to have a father like other children. He's feeling that he's different. I understand that he is going to have difficulties, but I also understand that all children have difficulties. So he doesn't have a father and his mother's a lesbian. So there are children whose parents are alcoholics and who fight and who are divorced. But we never lie to him. Whatever it is he needs to know, we tell him the truth. The important thing here is to give this kid the understanding that he is very loved.

PFLAG was my political milestone. I became what I would certainly call an activist in the movement. Marching in the Pride parade. Marching on Washington. I've been on television. I speak at colleges and schools. I wear a pink triangle on my pocketbook. A very bold pink triangle. I do it deliberately because I want people to see it. I want it in their face. I want them to ask me questions and they do. It never fails. They'll ask what it means and I tell them it means someone you care about or love is lesbian or gay. I'm in PFLAG because it's my opportunity to help other people along their path and to validate them and let them know that I know their pain and that I was them. That's what I tell them. I tell them, "I am you. I was there. I was a basket case." They need that. People have written me letters and called me and thanked me and made me feel I'm doing something for someone else. Helping them to make their life a little easier. My husband comes to all the meetings with me. He has been on television. We have marched together hand in hand at the Gay Pride parade. The first year the baby was born, we had him in a stroller dressed in purple and we marched as a family with banners and stuff.

It isn't always easy. There was a movement in the public school system a few years ago when they wanted to introduce textbooks where somebody had two mommies and two daddies. Now the school board was going nuts. They didn't want this although it also covered a grandmother that might be raising a child as well as interracial marriage. The reason for it was so children would not feel different from other children. During Show and Tell and stuff like that. The material, oddly enough, was really designed for the teachers so they could become more sensitive to diversity in the classroom. Not to give to the children. Father's Day, as one example. If Heather had two mommies, she didn't have to make something for her father and didn't have to feel embarrassed about it.

The school board held a meeting on what was called the Rainbow Curriculum and I decided to get up and speak. These people with narrow minds and fearful that if this information was introduced into the public school system, their children would be affected by it. They'd be influenced into thinking that it was okay to be gay. I thought they were going to kill me. That was the one time that I felt fearful for my daughter's safety. I never saw such hate in this day and age. I'm talking about the year 2000 with the information that's out there. They were so against this curriculum that they were screaming. They wanted to kill those of us who were courageous enough to get up there and talk. Ignorance. It was like they wanted to stone us. Take us back to the old biblical days.

So I'm an activist now. Somebody interviewed me at the Gay Pride March and I was in the *New York Times*. People came over to me and asked, "Is that you?" They didn't know my daughter was gay. Not because I kept it a secret, but there was no occasion to say anything. I said, "Yep, that's me. I have a lesbian daughter." Anytime I'm interviewed and it's been printed, I give my name. But you can't expect all parents or mothers to do that. I'm not angry at them. Most people are ashamed. They're in the closet. It's very complicated. It has a lot to do with who the mother is. Who she is as a person. Maybe she's very shy and reserved. It's your personality. My basic character is to fight for what I believe in. Once I believe in something, no matter what the issue is. It's who I am. Like fighting for choice. I once took my daughter for an abortion. I believe that my daughter should have the choice to have an abortion. If I really believe in it, I'm going to fight. I practically wanted to kill the people that were demonstrating against it.

If I knew then, when I was a young woman what I know now, I would have been a lesbian. This is how I see it. When I was a little girl, I was holding hands and playing with my little girlfriends and I loved them and they meant everything to me. Then boys got in the way during adolescence. We became competitive because all we cared about was being with boys. Boys separated us. As an older woman I'm coming back to my girlfriends. I love the women in my life. They're where my heart is. Knowing that they understand me and that they're hearing me.

You know that book, *Men are From Mars, Women are From Venus*? I think that men are really on a whole different wave length. I'm now seeing men in a very different way. Seeing them as having served a purpose. It was okay all the years I was raising my children and being so crazy in love with my husband and the hot sex thing with the hormones raging and all that. But now I want the women in my life back. I savor those relationships. I think that lesbian women have an advantage. They have the specialness of the connection to another woman that I don't have.

I'll tell you that the strange thing is I'm grateful to my daughter because I think that she made me more of a person. Had I not had her for a daughter, I would never have been as accepting, as giving a person, as out there, as politically active as I am. Not only for gays and lesbians. I see the world in a different way. She opened my heart and my mind to people. To ideas other than what I had been brought up with. If I hadn't had her, I would be nothing. If I only had average children, I would have just been an average person. I am so enriched by what she has allowed me to experience having been her mother. Having had the privilege of being her mother.

Marie, age sixty-three, was divorced and remarried. She attended college and had worked as an interior designer. She had three children. Her religious background was Catholic, but she called herself an agnostic. Marie found out that her daughter Angie was a lesbian in 1973 when she was seventeen and, at the time of the interview, was the mother of two young sons. Marie was supportive of abortion rights and the Women's movement. She was a member of PFLAG, marched in Gay Pride parades, and was an outspoken and public activist on behalf of LGBT civil rights, calling it her life's work. Marie lived in Brooklyn and was interviewed in 2000.

23

Judith

I HAVE A MUCH HAPPIER SON THAN I EVER DID A DAUGHTER

I FIRST THOUGHT OF MY DAUGHTER being a lesbian at age two. There were very obvious signs from the beginning. She wouldn't play with dolls. At eighteen months, she wanted to urinate standing up. At age twenty-seven months, when her brother was born, she only wanted to wear his clothing. And at age three, she was calling herself Fred. So I knew from a very early point that this child had very lesbian tendencies. What I considered to be butch.

Adam was very bright as a little girl. Very articulate, funny, and charming with a phenomenal vocabulary by the age of three. But adolescence was hell for him. He dressed in boy's clothing and he would not wear a bra. I did everything I could to try and make him more feminine and, of course, that was a problem. His peers thought he was strange and different so he was quite a loner. He spent a lot of time listening to music and I think that was a wonderful outlet for him.

She, my daughter, actually didn't come out until age twenty-nine when she called and told us that she felt she was bisexual. I, at that point, was relieved because I felt that the gay issue was very strong and it was something that she wasn't able to live with until she became bisexual. He had been married as a woman to a male and that marriage lasted three years. But it only took six weeks until he transitioned to transsexual and was identified wholly as a male. So this was all when he was twenty-nine.

Although he showed very masculine behavior from the beginning, I had never thought about transsexual. Even though I was aware of transsexualism, a light bulb just had never gone off that this could ever have been the case. Nor did my son give me any indication that he was trapped in the wrong body, or that he himself felt he was a male. When he told us, I understood transsexualism and knew exactly what he was saying. My immediate thoughts, feelings, and concerns were that I needed to have more knowledge. I needed to understand what was going on. My husband and I booked a flight to the East Coast where he was living and we met his support group which was the transsexual community. We had some pretty heavy duty, almost like therapy, sessions. There was a lot of rage. A lot of anger. I'm sure there still is a lot of anger directed at us and certainly at society. But we came back with a lot of information and knowing he had a terrific support system in place.

My husband and I actually were probably two of the most people that dealt with this very comfortably and easily. We were not in any pain. When he transitioned, it was actually a relief to both of us because we felt that we had an answer to all the pain and misery and suffering that this child had gone through all of his life. We were never really very happy with our daughter. We had a child that was not very likable. She never bonded with me and I did not have a good relationship with her. She always thought that she was an embarrassment to me. I was estranged from this person for several years and when he transitioned, it brought us back together again. So it actually healed our relationship once he transitioned. So for us, it was an awakening. It was a rejoicing. It was wonderful. What was difficult, of course, was slowly letting friends and family become aware of his transition. And how you do it and when, was always a concern for us. A big concern that both my husband and I have is the fact that my son identifies as a male homosexual and we're always fearful about the element of society who is so anti-gay that he could be in danger by associating with people or meeting people that are homophobic. That's really my only concern at this time.

When I came back home, I started looking for a support group for parents, friends, and family but found there was none. I started by calling a friend, an acquaintance actually, who I knew had a transsexual son and thought would be a perfect person to share this with—and who would need help and support. But this person wanted very little support. They had abandoned their child and did not want to talk about it. We were really rebuffed by reaching out to them. This was a family in our neighborhood, a professional family, and I was a little surprised that there was so much anger and rejection of this child.

There was a period of time when my husband went through the mourning of the loss of a daughter and that took approximately one year. Getting the pronouns right took about three or four months. I don't actually even talk about a daughter anymore. I talk about him as being my son even though I raised him as a girl. So it's a little unusual for me actually even to refer to Adam as a daughter. We've come to the point where we both feel that he was always our son. We just didn't know it. We understood that even though we were raising who we thought was a daughter, he was always a little boy.

My other son is very open and accepting, as is his wife and her family. We've had very few people that could not deal with this. So it really hasn't affected us in any way. In fact, most of my friends are proud of me and for my action in starting a support group for the trans community. I didn't plan on telling my eighty-five year old mother because I felt it wasn't necessary. But she kept asking me how my daughter was and if she was meeting anyone and I found myself so comfortable with the male pronouns that it was becoming more difficult to talk to her about it.

So when I went to see her, I told her that this child was dressing as a male and if she were to ever see her grandchild again, it would be as a male and that she had also changed her name to Adam. She thought about it and thought about it and looked at me and said, "Is she going to have surgery?" I answered, "Yes." Then she paused and looked at me and said, "A human being is a human being and we will always love her." It took her a little while to get the pronouns, but this mother of mine was totally accepting as was most of my family. I told this story at my mother's funeral and talked about my son transitioning to all the people who probably didn't know what a transsexual was. But I honored my mother by talking about unconditional love.

I talk to people only on a one-to-one basis when I felt the situation or circumstances were comfortable. When people were really concerned about my daughter and asked me continually about her. Not just casual acquaintances. If someone stopped and asked how were my kids, how is my daughter, I generally would say, "Fine, thank you and how are your kids?" I would say ninety-five per cent of our circle of friends certainly know about it and I'm very open about sharing it with my friends. I'm also quite active in a support group. I haven't made an announcement at the office nor do I feel it's necessary to tell the casual person on the street because it just takes too much time and energy to explain.

I am very warm and caring with people. I might put my hand out and touch them on the shoulder and tell them that it's something that they probably will never have to deal with. I tell them this is a situation that has really been a blessing in our life and that they don't have to feel sorry for us. People that feel it's a sin, I suppose, probably don't say anything to me. I'm sure people with very negative feelings aren't going to come up and approach me. But I feel the best thing I can do is be positive and happy and let people know that, for us, it was a blessing and not a situation that turned out to be a tragedy. I think that when people see how well we deal with it, they tend to change their attitude a little bit.

If I would change anything, and of course I would, I didn't listen enough to my child. I had a preconceived notion of who this person was. I wanted him to fit the mold of a daughter, even though it would have been a gay lesbian daughter. I put flowers in his room. I still had this picture of him as a female. I always wanted a daughter. But I don't have a daughter and I do feel that loss. I think had I listened more carefully, I probably could have picked up signs about the transsexual identity, but I think that my mind was pretty made up.

When he was fourteen, I did call a pediatric endocrinologist who was a friend of mine and I asked her to see my child because I said there was a lot of male behavior. Deep voice, irregular periods. I knew something was wrong, but this friend of mine just poo pooed the whole idea and said that he'll outgrow it and don't worry about it. I never pursued it with another doctor. I regret that deeply. But I would not have known how to find a gender therapist nor did I know that this was a gender identity problem so I really would not have known what to do with this adolescent. So yes, I do have regrets.

I was raised by a Jewish mother who was possessive, loving, and controlling, but really quite wonderful. Quite a wonderful caring mother, although smothering. I was raised as a secular Jew so I had no problem in feeling that this was not a sin, but an answer to a problem. So my spiritual and religious beliefs were never in question. In fact, it helped me. I went right away in the beginning to seek information. But I didn't know where to find it until I connected with PFLAG. Although they didn't have any answers, they were very accommodating in helping me to set up coordinators in every chapter so we now have—that is, in most chapters—a transsexual coordinator to help anyone that comes to PFLAG looking for answers on gender identity.

I have a wonderful story. My son was best friends with another girl in high school and the two of them were two of the brightest kids in the class. They were best friends although they were quite competitive with each other. Just prior to transitioning, he got a phone call from this guy who said, "Hi, this is Matt, do you remember me?" Adam didn't know who he was until he told him his female name. So it turned out that these two young girls both became transsexuals. Matt's family has never accepted him. He was pretty much one of the throwaways and it was very difficult for this young man to accept that his family would reject him totally.

I have a great deal of difficulty in handling parents that reject their children. If these parents are fundamentalists or living in a very narrow world—or living by what their neighbors think—well that dictates the outcome of their either accepting or rejecting their child. You can't change someone that has totally rejected or thrown away their children. They have to come to this on their own and if they change, all the more power to them. But it's very damaging and it's very painful for me to see. But I do think that education is probably the most powerful tool that we can give people. I often tell people in the transsexual community to move on. That it's okay to divorce your parents, to remember all the good that was there as they were growing up, and to find new families and new support.

197

I am a transgender coordinator in my area. I talk to a lot of parents about this and there is nothing more devastating or shame-filled than someone going through the transitioning of one gender to another. Society totally rejects it. They are made fun of to the point that a lot of these adolescents and young people are suicidal. I don't think that there is anything more devastating or more difficult than transitioning from one gender to another in our society. I do a lot of support one-on-one with other families. This week I got two phone calls, both from parents of female to males who were transitioning. One was fourteen and the other twenty. Last week we took out another couple for dinner and brought them back to our home and gave them a lot of information. My husband is also very involved and he will do anything he can to help a father understand what it's like for another father to have gone through the transitioning of a child. He's very accepting so I think that it's helpful for other men to see someone who is accepting and loving. He's a terrific role model. But it would probably be much more difficult for my husband to deal with losing a son and having a daughter. I think that that might have been a more difficult transition.

What I believe is that I think this happens in utero. They are born this way and they have no choice. But at some point in their lives, sometimes not until their forties or fifties—or possibly until their parents die that they become comfortable with transitioning and coming out to be the person they've always believed they truly were. This is not something that you can influence and I don't think it has anything to do with how they were raised. I feel very deeply about this. I do try to be less judgmental. I try to look at the soul of a person and not so much the exterior, but of course, with our society that's a little hard to do because whether you pass or not makes such a difference. For most male to females, well they don't pass as easily as FTMs and it's really hard to accept someone that is obviously very male looking dressed in female's clothing—so I do tend to still be a little judgmental.

I think parents of a gay child experience different emotions. It's certainly a different reaction than parents with a transgendered child. Sexual preference is only one part of the picture. I think transgendered is a much more complex part and much more difficult to deal with. The change of pronouns and having to deal with the transitioning from one gender to another. I can't think of anything that would be more difficult than that, although certainly there is a loss when you have a gay child because parents often feel deprived of having grandchildren. But it's really about that their expectations just may not be fulfilled. Something all parents have to deal with.

To me, it's like belonging to a club where I would never have got admission to before and it's a wonderful club. I have met some of the most interesting, loving, caring, and giving human beings that have ever walked on the earth. Transsexuals have been through so much pain in their lives that I don't know anyone who isn't kind, caring, and giving. They are just beautiful human beings and I feel honored that I am part of this community. Adam's very proud of me for what I'm doing with the transgender community in our town and I think that, at this point, there probably couldn't be a better relationship.

He looks terrific. He's five feet and two inches so obviously he's a very small male. His chest surgery was successful and wonderful. He walks around like a peacock. He is as happy as can be. What once was a selfish, uncaring, and self-centered female is now a happy, outgoing, unselfish, much more caring—and much more involved with the family—male. So yes, my son is a person who has finally found the answer to all the problems that besieged him all his life. We feel so much more positive about him. He is now with a male partner. He has bought a home. He's got a job and he has mainstreamed beautifully. He really is a wonderful example of a happy transitioned person who is living his life in the best way he knows how. The positive thing is having a child who is happy. I mean, isn't that what every parent wants for their child, their child to be happy? So I have a much happier son than I ever did a daughter.

Judith, age fifty-seven, was born in Canada. She was married, had attended college, and worked in sales and real estate. She had two children and identified herself as Jewish, but secular. Her child Amy—now Adam—was married and disclosed first as bisexual when he was twenty-nine in 1994, and then six weeks

*later as transgender. Judith was active in her local trans commu-
nity, started a local trans support group through* PFLAG, *and was
instrumental in setting up trans coordinators in regional* PFLAG
*chapters. She also coordinated an informational and support group
for parents and families of trans people through the Internet and
was a nationally known activist and leader in the transgender
rights movement. Judith lived in Illinois and was interviewed by
mail in 2001.*

24

Martha

JUST EXPECT TO SEE SOMEBODY THAT LOOKS LIKE YOUR FORMER DAUGHTER'S TWIN BROTHER

OUR DAUGHTER ELLEN—NOW BRIEN—lived pretty happily as a lesbian for eighteen years. He had a partner for eight years, although that relationship was going kind of going sour and they eventually broke up. When she came out as a transsexual, she said that when she was a teenager, she always wanted to be a gay guy like some of her good friends were. So I guess it began to itch again. He finally figured out that lesbian was not quite it and was thrilled to discover a transgender support group in his city and started attending meetings. I guess he quickly felt right at home and that was his path and my husband and I have no doubts, whatsoever, that this was right for him. We think he's happier, a little more assertive, and a little more stable. No partner, but everything else seems to be falling into place.

It was a complete shock both times. First, coming out as a lesbian. Then transgender. Both were okay intellectually. I was a social worker. We were Unitarians. Gay was fine. But when you have no idea that your kid is gay, I always say it's a kick in the gut and entirely different. Maybe it was 1975 or 1976 and, at that point, there wasn't anything really good to read or anyone to talk to, and very little in the way of support available. He said that we said all the right things. You know, we love you and it will work out and it's fine. And we proceeded not to talk about it for quite a few years. I know now that's a stage parents go through although they think they're very accepting. They just don't want to talk about it. Kind of a semi-denial. If we don't talk about it much, maybe it will go away.

I started leaking it out to close friends and I never had any bad reactions when I told anyone. It was okay in the Unitarian Church even back then, but I think it took us about ten years to really be able to talk about it. We kept hoping it would go away and we went through this guilt thing. If only we hadn't sent her to this college where there was this gay group. If I hadn't been a working mother and had spent more time with her. I did all that stuff to myself so I understand the guilt trip mothers go through. It's all part of the process.

Brien was quite ill from six months to a year and was very clingy, very whiny. She was hospitalized for a few days and it was terrible. In those days, parents couldn't stay with them and here's this one-year-old being left in a crib, in a cage really, for three days. So she grew up very clingy and when she came home, she wouldn't let me out of her sight. I think it left some almost permanent scars. Then by the time she was a year old, I was six months pregnant and our second kid was born. So that was a hard year for us.

I was certainly more protective of this child and that probably explains why when she came out, my first thought was, who will take care of her? She'd never have anybody, a husband, to take care of her. Then somewhere down the line I started thinking she'll never be a mother. She'll never have children. She'll miss the greatest things in life and I was sad about that. When she finally got a partner, we were glad. But when we had our next family reunion, I hoped that she wasn't going to bring her. I wasn't ready to deal with all of our relatives. But they both came and to have the whole clan not bat an eye and to accept them both, and for it to be real obvious and just fine with everybody, well that was a benchmark. We didn't hold a press release or make an announcement, but it was official.

I began to become active in the gay movement about the time I retired and was living in a new city, bereft of friends and family and work that I loved. I tried several organizations and ended up starting a PFLAG chapter. A couple of years later I became a regional director and was traveling around starting other chapters and working with existing chapters and so forth. A natural for a social worker and a woman who didn't like to stay home. Eventually, I became president of my state's PFLAG chapter and became very involved in the gay community. My husband and I are close. We agree on a lot of things, but we've different temperaments. I think my activism is part of how I made the marriage work because if I didn't, I would be going stir crazy. So this was an excuse for me to get out and do things and he was happy kind of staying at home.

I think I went stir crazy when I was home with three children. By the time we'd been married four years, we had three babies and two of them were chronically ill for a period of time with a lot of crying. We moved lots and one developed nightmares—night terror, actually is what it was. We had a terrible, really rough time when the children were small. So I was very glad to kind of scoop them off to school. I wasn't going to cry when they went off and then my mother-in-law came and stayed with us and I went back to school.

I was a pretty liberal and laissez-faire mother. Dr. Spock was about the only book I ever read. When it came to mothering, I don't think I had much of a philosophy. It wasn't like I'd considered different kinds of child-rearing or how I was going to educate the children or anything. I let them try a lot of things. We let them taste any kind of alcohol around. I let them do their own thing and I think it worked out. None of them drink or smoke or do drugs and they were very good students and they're all good citizens. I wish I had had more patience with them when they were little. I wish I could have just held them more because I have a great yearning to have those little three and four year old tots back in my lap right now. It's really too bad. I always think that mothering comes in such overdoses and then they're gone. Then you're a wreck with regrets forever. So I wish I'd saved some of those moments that were too many back then and had some of them now.

I knew I'd never wanted to be exactly like my mother. I don't think I ever had total respect for her and I wasn't ever real close to her. She never went to college. She was a home mother and never did anything very particular with her life. She ran a beautiful home and she was a good cook and she was always there for us and I think she was a good wife and mother. That was her generation. But somehow that didn't impress me. I knew I wanted to do more than that. I knew I would be going to college and that I could pick a career. But my mother was totally devoted to doing everything she could for me. She took me to concerts. I had all kinds of dancing lessons and singing lessons and piano lessons. I don't think I was as devoted a mother. I was into my own career. Kind of let the kids grow up on their own. We had nice family vacations. We played a lot together at home. I can remember everybody had a pot and a spoon and we had our own family parades around the house and we did a lot of playgrounds. We traded kids back and forth with other families.

I don't think Brien had the excruciating discomfort that a lot of transsexuals will tell you they suffered. That, as a child, they would go to bed praying every night they'd wake up in the morning and either a penis would be gone or one would appear or something like that. They knew from very young that something was all wrong and that everyday getting up and putting on their clothes was like being in drag and nobody knew who they were and they were just miserable. I don't think our kid had that level of angst and dysphoria. But it was certainly an itch that persisted and reoccurred and she finally had to do something about it.

She probably figured it out for herself, or himself, around six months before she broke it to us. She did tell her sister first. I'd been to one transgender workshop at PFLAG and I even told some people that this was pretty interesting and wanted to know more about it. I was probably as ready as any mother could be. You know, to be a social worker and a Unitarian. I was already interested in the issue, having worked with hundreds of parents who have been through the kind of grief process that is associated with finding out your kid is in any kind of sexual minority. So there was a lot more support the second time around and I think we went through the grief process in about three weeks. Right after he came out, I attended a transgender workshop at the PFLAG national convention and then a second one the next year where some of us announced that we were parents of trans. I said that I was looking for other parents to talk to, and six of us pulled our chairs out in the hall and that was the beginning of the Transgender Network. We pretty soon had an e-mail list with one hundred people on it where we could ask questions and educate each other.

I didn't know what the change would mean and was reassured that he would still remember all his past and that past relationships don't disappear and that he would still have the same sense of humor and the same likes and dislikes. That was a comfort and I found it comforting when one of his friends said that waiters now called him sir. That was a benchmark. And then a trans man that I was e-mailing was talking about how he could come out to his parents and I told him that we were going out to see Brien and I had no idea what he looked like or what to expect. And he said, "Well, just expect to see somebody that looks like your former daughter's twin brother." That was very comforting. Something to hang onto.

Brien's now on hormones. First, the typical Harry Benjamin protocol and referral to a psychiatrist who started the hormonal therapy. At the first interview, he gave our kid a hard time and Brien called me and said, "What do you suppose is wrong with this psychiatrist? He's supposed to be good at this sort of thing and he just gave me a terrible time." I said, "I'll bet he's just testing you out. Go back and tell him you're not going to be put off." For once, mother was right. She went back and the psychiatrist did indeed administer the first hormone shot and now Brien is doing his own shots. He did those every two weeks for a number of years and now he's down to three weeks for the rest of his life.

He's had what they call top surgery and a hysterectomy. A lot of female-to-males do not go for the genital surgery because it's very expensive, very invasive, a lot of skin grafting involved, and you cannot create a penis that does all the things you would like it to do. You can pee out of the end of it and that's about it. He passes very well. Although most trans men are shorter than the average female, and most males to females are taller than the average male, our kid was lucky. He's about five feet, ten inches and makes, I think, a very credible looking man. He's not out at work and so he does pass very well as a man. He's stockier, his neck is thicker. He's put on weight. He's very proud of his receding hairline. He doesn't have a lot of facial hair, which he would probably love to have. I'm told that dark-haired people do better with the facial hair than blondes and he's brunette, sort of. He's more serious, happier.

When he started to transition, he kind of pulled away from the family and I felt worse about that. He was not in touch for a while and it was very difficult. I felt rejected for a year or two while he was transitioning. In my head, I knew that maybe he just needed that space. That he wasn't quite comfortable with his halfway status and needed to work that through himself. But that was probably more painful to me than the gender transition. He needed his space to get comfortable and I was probably asking more questions than he wanted to deal with. And so I went elsewhere with my questions. I, by then, was developing my own transgender hotline and e-mail list where I got my basic education. It was about half parents and half trans folks and so you could put out a question and get a variety of answers or opinions and that was just very, very helpful and comforting. Educational. Supportive. All that.

Now, I feel like he's back in the fold and we're probably closer to him again than we are to the other two children. I do relate to him differently than I did when he was my daughter. I think I am less protective. I've had to learn to let go. We had to redo that relationship and I think that his pulling away for a while kind of broke our—well, perhaps too close, maybe an enmeshment relationship. I think we probably have a better relationship now. A different one anyway. He's single again and we've spent more vacation time together and that sort of thing. He's got some house construction projects going and my husband knows how to do that stuff. So he goes out there and they're kind of man-to-man now. Doing the electrical work and the pipes. No problem with his siblings. One's husband made a few negative comments to me one time. I think he thought this was just like an adolescent aberration, but he's okay with it now. My husband and Ellen were particularly close. But he's a man of few words who never can describe a feeling so I'll never know how hard it was, or how easy it was for him. But he's now comfortable with it and proud of Brien and loves to tell people how much happier Brien is and this was the best thing for him.

I sort of learn more when I can listen in when other people are asking him questions. We did a little videotape together when PFLAG was trying to crank out a trans family tape. So Brien, my husband,

and I put ourselves in front of a camcorder with two lesbian women. They were his only friends left from pre-transition and were asking him questions. Brien said, "You know, I used to think I was happy. I had a partner. I had a house, but now I know what it is to be really happy." And I thought that was very touching. I don't think he's quite sure about his sexual orientation. My experience is that most trans folks are still attracted to the same kind of people they were before. Somebody else asked him if he was straight or gay and I was glad he asked that because I couldn't. And Brien said, "I don't know. I think I'll just try and see what works."

His name change was hard. But the pronouns! It was much harder to start using the new pronouns. Pronouns seem so much more, so much more clearly the other gender. The name, Brien was quite different than Ellen and I hated giving up the name we really loved. But to say he and him and his is much harder. And you know every once in a while, even though it's been over five years now, I still slip. Even when I'm talking to my husband, I refer every once in a while to her.

How parents react has a lot to do with their reference group, their religion. I think it has to do with just a liking to explore new ideas and new people and new places. Those are the parents that I think make it. The parents who are scared of life, who shut themselves off, have a very limited circle of friends, and very limited closed ways of looking at life and the world are the parents who I think have real problems. I think it also has to do with whether there are other children and other children with grandchildren and extended family and what's going on with them. But I think the main one is a basic personality factor that has to do with openness and adventurousness.

I have come to a different worldview. I do a talk called, *Nature Loves a Continuum*. I don't see the world in dichotomies. Since Aristotle, who believed that a thing was either A or not A, we've viewed the world in dichotomies. We are tall or short, fat or thin, successful or unsuccessful. Certainly it's taken us a long time to admit to anything besides straight and gay. I mean bi's have had a hard time from both sides and at least male and female was something we could count on. Right? No! The last dichotomy is crumbling away. I see the world differently than I used to. I see us as more on a continuum which makes us all more connected than at different places. It was a little like a religious awakening. I just feel more connected to everything. The whole world is more continuous and gender is many faceted, amazing, wonderful, and fascinating.

Once you get it, you never want to go back and give up this learning. We say, in PFLAG, that parents go through this grief process. But unlike Kübler-Ross, there is one more stage. And that's celebration. We think our kids are fabulous just the way they are! We wouldn't change them if we could. They wouldn't be the same and we wouldn't want to go back to that pre-state of not knowing and not understanding. It also takes a parent to get past their own inner turmoil and see that it's the kid's happiness that is what's going on with the kid. Some parents get stuck with, "Why are you doing this to me?" It's a *me* thing. We probably all go through that a little bit, but we have to get past that.

I'm way out and so is my husband. Our home telephone number is the hook line for the local PFLAG group and now my home telephone number and our address and our e-mail address is on the back of 25,000 of those little books on trans floating around the country. I've written for many, many journals and my own books have my address and phone and e-mail on the back. Only slightly public, huh? You can't get much more out than that.

Parents come into PFLAG and they talk about their sons who have just come out as gay and say they feel like they've lost their son. We pat them on the back and say, "There, there, it's the same son. The same daughter. You just didn't know this particular side." But we really did lose a beautiful daughter. We have a great new son but we still miss our daughter sometimes. She was a very pretty, very sweet and loving lady. Other mothers and I have talked about this too. We're out there rah-rah-ing our new sons and organizing and on our soapboxes and writing and speaking a lot, but when we get off in the corner together, we miss our daughters.

Martha, age seventy-one, was married and a retired social worker. She identified herself as Unitarian. Her child Ellen—now Brien—disclosed as a lesbian at age eighteen and then as transgender at age thirty-six in 1993. Martha was active in the civil rights and gay movements and a nationally known published author on families of transgender people and activist in the transgender civil rights movement. She lived in Virginia and was interviewed in 2001.

Appendices

The Interviews

Each interview began with the reading of the Confidentiality and Questions Statement followed by an Introductory Statement in which each mother was asked to tell the story of how she learned that her child was a lesbian—or identified as transgender. If her child identified as transgender, a statement on language was read and each mother asked to respond to a series of Initial Questions regarding transition.

Following each mother's story—if not addressed—a series of questions were asked based upon an Interview Questions Guide informed by the literature on parents of lesbians (Borhek; Fairfield and Hayward; Muller; Rafkin), FTMs, (Brown and Rounsley; Cromwell; Devor), narratives written by parents of FTMs (Boenke), and information distributed by parents' organizations. The Confidentiality and Questions Statement, Introductory Statement, and Interview Questions Guide were mailed to the mothers who could not be interviewed in person (along with the Initial Questions to the mothers of transgender children) with instructions to tape their story, respond to all questions, and return their tape to me.

Confidentiality and Questions Statement

Before beginning our interview, I would like to know if you have any concerns regarding confidentiality of information. If you have

210

particular concerns, what would help you to feel that you and your child will be fully protected? Also, please feel free to ask any questions that you may have about this study.

Mothers of Lesbian Daughters

Introductory Statement

I am interested in understanding your experience when you learned that your daughter was a lesbian. In particular, I would like to understand how you felt when she first told you, and if—and how—your feelings, thinking, and perspectives changed over time. I would like you to tell your particular story and to think back on the circumstances, how it began, and what happened along the way. I would like to know the milestone events or process that might have led to changes in thinking, reactions, and feelings, and what it is like for you now. I understand that talking about this might be difficult and that your story may be a complicated one. However, I want to hear about it as it happened so I can understand it as your story as well as the story of your relationship with your child. I will interact with you as you talk and ask questions throughout so that I can be certain that I understand and am clear about what you are telling me (if interviewed in person).

Interview Questions Guide

I. Learning that a daughter is a lesbian
1. Please describe the circumstances when your daughter told you that she was a lesbian.
2. Did you understand what she was telling you? What were your immediate thoughts, feelings, and concerns?
3. How did she tell you? What did she say? Did you know before she told you? Were there prior signs or indications?
4. What was it like for you to hear that your daughter was a lesbian?
5. What happened afterwards? What did you do? What did your daughter do?

6. What were your feelings about your daughter then? How do you feel about her now?

7. What was your picture of your daughter's life before she told you that she was a lesbian?

8. How do you picture her life now?

II. Self and family

1. What was going on in your life then?

2. Did her father know? What were his feelings? Did this affect your relationship? If so, how?

3. What was your daughter's relationship like with her father?

4. If other children, what was their reaction then? Their reaction now?

5. If other children, what is your relationship with them like?

6. How did (and does) your daughter's lesbianism affect family relationships?

7. How has it affected you and your extended family? Friendships? Social life? Work life?

8. Did you have particular concerns or fears regarding yourself, your family, or your daughter?

III. Telling others

1. Who did you tell? Who knows now?

2. What has it been like telling immediate family? Extended family? Friends?

3. How did you decide who to tell and when to tell?

4. How did you manage or cope with difficult or negative responses?

IV. Relationship with your daughter

1. What was your relationship with your daughter like before she told you that she was a lesbian?

2. How often was there contact? Who typically initiated contact?

3. What was your relationship like afterwards? Your relationship now?

4. Are you close now? Did the kind of relationship you had with your daughter change after she came out?

V. Motherhood

1. Did you have a philosophy or set of beliefs on the kind of mother you wanted to be?

2. What do you think your strengths were as a mother of young children? Your strengths now?

3. Would you change anything about your mothering when your child or children were young or adolescent? Are there any regrets?

4. Can you tell me about your own mother's style of mothering? What did you like? What did you wish were different?

VI. Your daughter

1. Can you tell me a little about your daughter. What was she like as a child? An adolescent?

2. Is she in a relationship? Your feelings about her partner(s)?

3. How has her life changed?

4. Does she seem to be the same person as before? If not, how is she different? If so, how does this affect you?

5. Have you discussed being interviewed with her? If so, how did she react?

VII. Your beliefs

1. Did your religious, spiritual, or political beliefs influence accepting a lesbian daughter?

VIII. Lesbianism

1. What were your views, beliefs, and values on homosexuality prior to knowing that your daughter was a lesbian? How did you understand or explain it?

2. Did you seek out information on lesbianism? Where? Are your views on homosexuality and lesbianism different now?

3. Did you know any lesbians or gay men prior to your

daughter's disclosure? Did you meet any lesbians or gay men afterwards?

4. If so, what has it been like meeting lesbians and gay men?

5. What would you like to know about lesbianism or lesbians' lives?

6. Are there any rewards or positives to having a lesbian daughter?

7. Is there anything in your experience—beliefs, values, or upbringing—that helped or hindered accepting your daughter's lesbianism?

8. Is there anything that would help to make your daughter's lesbianism more acceptable?

IX. Activism/Final questions

1. Are you a member of a parents' LGBT support group? If so, what is it like attending meetings?

2. If a member of a parents' support group, what helped you or were the factors that led you to join a support group of parents of LGBT children? Is your child's father involved?

3. If engaged in LGBT activism, what helped you or were the factors that led you to become an "ally" and active in support of civil rights of LGBT people? Is her father involved?

4. Do you think your experience as a mother of a lesbian daughter has been typical or atypical?

5. How do you picture the experience of a mother whose child (adult or adolescent) tells her that she or he is planning to transition to male or female?

6. What do you think of mothers or family members who are unable to accept a gay or transgender child? What do you think are the characteristics of people who reject a gay or transgender child?

7. Are there any other questions that I did not ask that you would like to address?

Mothers of Transgender Children

Introductory Statement

I am interested in understanding your experience when you learned that your child was in the process of, or intending to, transition to male. In particular, I would like to understand how you felt when he first told you, and if—and how—your feelings, thinking, and perspectives changed over time. I would like you to tell your particular story and to think back on the circumstances, how it began, and what happened along the way. I would like to know the milestone events or process that might have led to changes in thinking, reactions, and feelings, and what it is like for you now. I understand that talking about this might be difficult and that your story may be a complicated one. However, I want to hear about it as it happened so I can understand it as your story as well as the story of your relationship with your child. I will interact with you as you tell it, and ask questions throughout so that I can be certain that I understand and am clear about what you are telling me (if interviewing in person).

Language

I will refer to your child as a child or as a daughter prior to transition—and then as a child or a son after transition. Please let me know if you have any other preference as to language now and as we talk during the interview (if interviewing in person).

Initial Questions

What steps has your child completed? Where is he in the process of transitioning to male?
- Passing through dress/presentation?
- Hormonal injections?
- Reassignment surgery? What kind?
- Hysterectomy?
- Any other surgery or cosmetic procedures?
- Are there additional steps planned?

Interview Questions Guide

I. Learning that a child is planning to transition

1. Please describe the circumstances when your child told you that he had begun, or was thinking about, or planning to transition to male?

2. What was his then status in terms of the transitioning process?

3. Did you know before he told you? Were there prior signs or indications?

4. How did he tell you? What did he say?

5. How did you understand what he was telling you? Your reaction? What was it like for you to hear what he was saying?

6. What were your immediate thoughts, feelings, and concerns? Did you have particular concerns or fears regarding yourself, your family, or your child?

7. What happened afterwards? What did you do? What did your child do?

8. What were your feelings about your child then? How do you feel about him now?

9. What was your picture of your child's life before he told you that he identified as male?

10. How do you picture his life now?

II. Self and family

1. What was going on in your life then?

2. Did his father know? What were his feelings? Has this affected your relationship? If so, how?

3. What was your child's relationship like with his father?

4. If other children, what is your relationship with them like? Your child's relationship with his siblings?

5. If other children, what were their reactions? Has this affected family relationships?

6. How has this affected you and extended family relationships? Friendships? Social life? Work?

III. Telling others

1. Who did you tell? Who knows now?

2. What has it been like telling immediate family? Extended family? Friends?

3. How did you decide who to tell and when to tell?

4. How did you manage or cope with difficult or negative responses?

IV. Relationship with your child

1. What was your relationship with your child like before he told you about transitioning?

2. How often was there contact? Who typically initiated contact?

3. What was your relationship like afterwards? Your relationship now?

4. Are you close now? Did the kind of relationship you had with your child change after he transitioned?

V. Changes

1. Can you talk about your feelings and reactions as your child transitioned.

2. Presenting as male?

3. If and when he began to take hormones?

4. Pre and post surgery?

5. Other changes?

VI. Mothering

1. Did you have a philosophy or particular beliefs on the kind of mother you wanted to be?

2. What do you think your strengths were as a mother of young children? Your strengths now?

3. Would you change anything about your mothering when your child or children were young or adolescent? Do you have any regrets?

4. Can you tell me about your own mother's style of mothering? What did you like? What did you wish were different?

VII. **Your child**

1. Can you tell me a little about your child? What was he like as a young child? An adolescent?

2. Is he in a relationship? What is his sexual orientation? Your feelings about this? Your feelings about his partner(s)?

3. How has his life changed?

4. Does he seem to be the same person as before? If not, how is he different? If so, how does this affect you?

5. Have you discussed being interviewed with him? How did he react?

VIII. **Beliefs**

1. Did your religious, spiritual, or political beliefs influence acceptance of a transgender child?

IX. **Transgenderism**

1. What were your views, beliefs, and values on transgenderism and FTM trans identity prior to knowing that your child identified as male and was planning to transition?

2. How did you understand or explain it?

3. Did you seek out information on transgenderism and FTMs? If so, how did you obtain this information? Are your views different now?

4. What would you like to know about transition and FTM trans peoples' lives?

5. Is there anything that would help to make your child's transition to male more acceptable?

6. Are there any rewards or positives to having a FTM trans child?

7. Would you feel differently if you had a son who transitioned to female?

8. Would your experience have been different if you became aware that your child identified as male when he was a young child or adolescent?

9. Did you know any trans people prior to your child's disclosure?

10. Is there anything in your experience—beliefs, values, upbringing which helped or hindered accepting transition?

11. What has it been like meeting other trans individuals? Reactions?

x. Activism/Final questions

1. Are you a member of PFLAG or a parents of trans people support group? If so, what is it like attending meetings?

2. If a member of any group, what helped you or were the factors that led you to join a support group of parents of LGBT children? Is his father involved?

3. If engaged in transgender activism, what helped you or were the factors which led you to become active in support of trans people and their civil rights? Is his father active?

4. Do you think your experience as a mother of a FTM trans person has been typical or atypical?

5. How do you picture the experience of a mother whose child (adult or adolescent) tells her that she is a lesbian?

6. What do you think of mothers or family members who are unable to accept a gay or trans child? What would you think are the characteristics of people who reject a gay or transgender child?

7. Is there anything that would help to make your child's transition to male more acceptable?

8. Are there any other questions that I did not ask that you would like to address?

Sarah F. Pearlman was selected by the American Psychological Association Society for the Psychological Study of Lesbian, Gay, Bisexual, and Transgender Issues as the recipient of the 2011 Award for Distinguished Professional Contribution. Employed for many years as an Associate Professor in the Doctoral Program in Clinical Psychology at the University of Hartford, Sarah is now Associate Professor Emeritus. She lives in Boston and is active in LGBT elder organizations.